Classic British Prop

There are few sights and sounds in aviation more evocative than a classic propliner in full flight… and there was no better time and place to witness these glorious machines than in post-war Britain. This was the golden age of the props, when the aircraft that plied the airways represented the zenith of piston-powered technology, hotly pursued by the new 'fangled' turboprop. But sadly the glory was to be short lived…

The post-war years were an exciting but troubled time for the British airliner industry. It was battling to wrest control of the skies away from the dominance of the giant US conglomerates, but it was hamstrung by decisions made by the infamous Brabazon Committee. Set up in 1943 to safeguard the very survival of the airliner industry in peacetime, the Committee's thinking was both expansive and conservative, though misguided on both counts. For a committee buried in the 1940s, jet travel was just too futuristic to be fully trusted. Instead it championed the proven piston-engine, backed up, somewhat reluctantly, by the 'go-between' turboprop, a hybrid of both propeller and jet power. Unwittingly, it had struck the death knell for the future of the British aviation industry. But in the meantime, it left us with a legacy of wonderfully exotic machines that demonstrated the very best and worst of British ingenuity and eccentricity. Without Lord Brabazon and his committee, we would not have seen the like of the world's first true 'jumbo' in the shape of the narcissistically-named Brabazon, the eight-engined giant that was an engineering marvel, yet outmoded at the same time. Another gargantuan crowd pleaser was the Princess flying boat, a machine that again was doomed even before the first rivet had been hammered into its sublime hull. But it was not all bad. Vickers produced a true record-breaking winner in its beautiful Viscount, the world's first turboprop airliner to enter service. And who could not be impressed by the majesty of the Britannia, an aircraft so divine that it virtually named itself? Meanwhile, the British manufacturers were busy producing a plethora of imaginative propeller-driven aircraft to supply the burgeoning number of airlines around the world. Many filled a niche market, serving 'parts that other aircraft could not reach', while others strove to be the next DC-3, a ubiquitous jack of all trades. But the window of opportunity was brief… competition was hotting up (literally) and the first generation of pure jet airliners quickly seduced the masses. The elitism of air travel was no more and the throbbing sound of the big propliner died alongside it, the dinosaurs of another era. But despite their antiquity, or perhaps because of it, there is one characteristic that all the propliners of old had, that the current crop of computer-generated machines would die for… charisma. Now that is what makes a true classic.
Allan Burney

AVIATION ARCHIVE SERIES

The age of the propliners may be long gone, but the nostalgia lives on and this issue of 'Aviation Archive' presents a pictorial tribute to some true British classics. For some, the word 'propliner' relates to piston power, but with the passage of time it has more commonly been applied to any aircraft that has a 'big fan' bolted onto the front of it. In the interest of variety, it is the latter parameter that we have adopted in 'Classic British Propliners'. Under the 'classic' moniker we have chronologically featured the main types constructed after the war that were either built for, or saw service with, a British airline. Hence we get the opportunity to begin with the delightfully idiosyncratic Bristol Freighter and end in grand style with the mighty Shorts Belfast. As ever, the photographs have been carefully selected out of the extensive 'Aeroplane Archive' for their historic and rarity value. The images are complemented by 'period' cutaways from the talented pens of the 'Flight' and 'Aeroplane' artists of the era and by contemporary profiles by Andy Hay and Rolando Ugolini.

Bibliography: *The Brabazon Committee and British Airliners 1945-1960* by Mike Phipp; *British Airliner Prototypes since 1945* by Stephen Skinner

Aviation Archive Series
Classic British Propliners
- **Editor:** Allan Burney • **Design:** Key Studio
- **Publisher and Managing Director:** Adrian Cox • **Executive Chairman:** Richard Cox • **Commercial Director:** Ann Saundry • **Group Editor:** Nigel Price
- **Distribution:** Seymour Distribution Ltd +44 (0)20 7429 4000 • **Printing:** Warners (Midlands) PLC, The Maltings, Manor Lane, Bourne, Lincs PE10 9PH.

Classic British Propliners

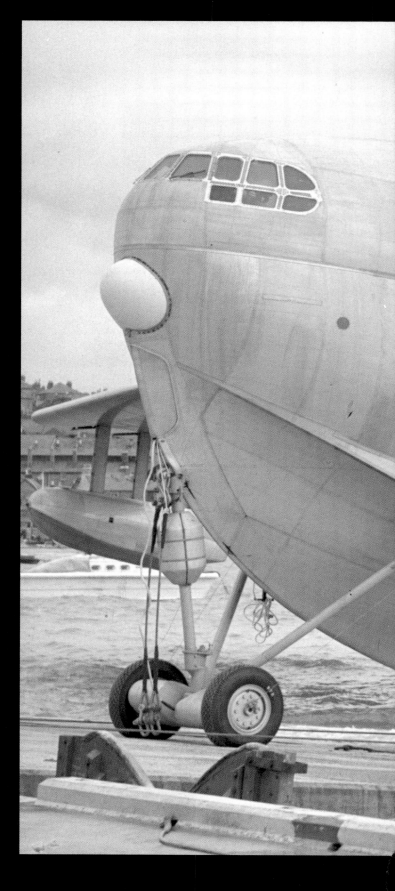

Bristol 170 Freighter

There was something quintessentially British about the rugged no-nonsense Bristol Freighter. Its large clamshell doors allowed it to swallow all manner of cargo, but perhaps its best-known use was as an air ferry to carry cars and their passengers over relatively short distances, a specialised niche that it was able to exploit for nigh on 50 years.

The Bristol 170 Freighter (and its Wayfarer passenger variant) grew out of the need for a wartime military transport that could fly vehicles and supplies in and out of rough airstrips. It was also designed as a stop-gap project to provide work for the Bristol company while the Bristol Brabazon was under development. Subsequently, the Air Ministry expressed interest in the project and two prototypes were ordered on the condition that the design was modified so that the aircraft could carry a British Army 3-ton truck. Of all-metal construction, it was to be a

twin-engined high-wing monoplane with large twin nose-doors to facilitate loading and unloading of cargo. The square-section fuselage was clear of internal obstructions and the flight deck was above the load space, accessed via a fixed ladder on the side of the cargo bay.

The prototype, registered G-AGPV, was first flown at Filton on 2 December 1945 by Cyril Uwins. He found it generally satisfactory, but asked for the tailplane to be lowered and increased in span to enable the aircraft to be trimmed to fly 'hands off' over a wide range of centre of gravity positions. The second prototype and the first 34-seat Wayfarer, registered G-AGVB, first flew on 30 April 1946, and began proving flights in the colours of Channel Islands Airways. After a number of

Bristol Freighter Mk 32	
Crew:	Two
Length:	73ft 4in (22.4m)
Wingspan:	108ft (32.92m)
Height:	25ft (7.62m)
Wing area:	1487ft² (138.13m²)
Empty weight:	29,950lb (13,404kg)
Gross weight:	44,000lb (19,958kg)
Powerplant:	2 × Bristol Hercules 734 14-cylinder sleeve-valve radial piston engine, 1,980hp each
Maximum speed:	225mph (362km/h)
Range:	820 miles (1,320km)
Service ceiling:	24,500ft (7,470m)

*Below: **Bristol Freighter Mk 31M G-BISU was operated by Instone Airline at Stansted, Essex, UK. This was an ex-RNZAF aircraft that flew its first charter flight on 3 August 1981 delivering two racehorses to Deauville. Re-registered as C-FDFC, in 1996 it crashed on take-off with the crew escaping, but was essentially a write-off. The captain reported that the aircraft entered a severe yaw after take-off, which was uncontrollable despite use of full opposite aileron and rudder control.***

G-BISU

*Left: **The unmistakable gaping mouth of the Bristol Freighter frames the Filton production line. Note the access ladder and hatch that provided the pilots with access to their lofty perch.***

demonstration flights around the world, the Bristol 170 entered full production at Filton, near Bristol.

Of the 214 Bristol Type 170s built, the best-known of all the versions was the Mk 32 with a lengthened fuselage, ordered by Silver City Airways. This version could accommodate two or three cars and 23 passengers. Apart from the large numbers of commercial versions which were supplied for use in all parts of the world for a variety of duties, the Type 170 was also produced as a military transport and served with the RAAF, RCAF (Mk 31 freighter version), the Pakistan Air Force and the RNZAF. The latter ordered 12 Mk 31M Freighters in the late 1940s and these ranged far and wide throughout the Far-East, including operating a military shuttle service for allies in Thailand during the Vietnam War.

The last two Freighters were delivered in 1958, one to New Zealand in February and the last aircraft to Dan-Air in March 1958. The New Zealand aircraft was delivered to Straits Air Freight Express (SAFE), which eventually operated one of the largest fleets of the type. One of the lengthened aircraft, registered G-AMWA, had 60 seats fitted and was known as a Super Wayfarer.

In a rather sad post-script to a much-loved type, 68 of the 214 Freighters built were destroyed or damaged beyond economical repair in accidents. At least 45 of these were fatal, resulting in the deaths of at least 385 passengers and crew.

Above: *An atmospheric scene at Le Touquet with an Armstrong Whitworth car being driven up the ramp of a Silver City Bristol Freighter. G-AGVC was actually the third example built, and the first to be fitted with fully operating nose doors. It inaugurated the Lympne-Le Touquet car ferry for Silver City Airways in July 1948 (presumably when this photograph was taken), before joining other Bristol 170s on the Berlin Airlift. In the early 1960s it was sold to Manx Airlines, but was written off at Ronaldsway on 30 June 1962.*

Far left: *In search of black gold. The adaptability of the Bristol 170 was put to good use by Hunting Aerosurveys that fitted out G-AICM with a survey camera and over a ton of photographic equipment in addition to survey operating gear. The aircraft had Perspex observation panels fitted in the nose doors and was equipped with oxygen apparatus for use at altitudes of up to 22,000ft. One of its first uses was to survey potential oil-bearing terrain in Iran.*

Left: *The horse-racing world was quick to recognise the advantages of transporting its thoroughbreds by air. Here Australian champion Attley is a bit hesitant to enter the gaping mouth of Bristol 170 G-AIMC at Melbourne for the 1,000 mile flight to Brisbane on 1 June 1947. Named Merchant Venturer, 'Mike Charlie' was Bristol's company demonstrator Freighter IA and was on a worldwide sales tour when it was damaged beyond repair at Wau, New Guinea on 23 October 1947. While on charter to Qantas, it was parked at the top of Wau's 1:12 gradient airstrip after landing, but the park brake cable failed and it rolled backwards down the runway and off the lower end into a deep ditch.*

Above right: *The hold of the Bristol Freighter was deceptively large and could transport large cars of the day, such as this classic 1953 Simca Aronde, with plenty of room to spare.*

Right: *It was not just cars and racehorses that the Bristol Freighter could devour. Here a Sycamore helicopter becomes its latest 'meal' in an impressive display at the Farnborough Air Show.*

Handley Page Hermes

The Hermes was the first British postwar airliner built to modern standards to go into service. Closely related to Handley Page's Hastings, 29 were built, serving briefly with BOAC in the early 1950s and later with several charter airlines until withdrawn from service in 1964. It had the distinction of beginning life as a 'tail dragger' before later variants were fitted with a more modern tricycle undercarriage.

With World War 2 drawing to a close, Handley Page turned its attention towards constructing a new civil and military transport aircraft, based on the wing of the Halifax bomber mated to a new fuselage and a single fin. A contract was received from the RAF to develop a military transport named the Hastings, and a civilian counterpart based on the same design became an obvious companion. Thus the Hermes was born. Starting life as a taildragger, the Hermes had an inauspicious start when the first prototype G-AGSS crashed during its maiden flight on 2 December 1945, killing both crew. When work was resumed on the second prototype, it was decided to lengthen the fuselage by 15ft

Right: The interior of the Hermes was very modern for its time.

Below: Hermes IV, G-ALDI Hannibal in better days. Although a graceful aircraft, sadly the Hermes was not fuel efficient and was quickly withdrawn from BOAC service. This aircraft's last operator was Silver City Airways before it was scrapped at Stansted in 1952.

and redesignate the aircraft HP74 Hermes II. Successful testing of the Hermes II led to the development of the HP81 Hermes IV, the definitive production version, which primarily differed by having a tricycle landing gear, more powerful Hercules engines and a slightly re-configured fuselage in accordance with customer BOAC's wishes. Some 25 were ordered for the carrier's African services. Although the first Hermes IV (registered G-AKFP) flew on 5 September 1948, and production built up quickly, the early aircraft were overweight, partly due to the use of Hastings components, and were initially rejected by BOAC.

The Hermes IV finally entered service with BOAC on 6 August 1950, taking over from the Avro York on the West Africa service from London Heathrow to Accra via Tripoli, Kano and Lagos, with services to Kenya and South Africa commencing before the end of the year. The standard interior layout allowed for a crew of five with 40 passengers, although a maximum of 63 passengers could be carried.

After only four years BOAC replaced the Hermes fleet with Canadair Argonauts as the Hermes had a tendency of flying tail-down, which increased drag, reduced speed and increased fuel consumption. Some did re-enter service in July 1954 following the grounding of the de Havilland Comet, before being retired again in December.

This was not the end of the Hermes in airline service, however, as surplus aircraft were sold to independent charter airlines, with Airwork purchasing four in 1952, and others being operated by Britavia and Skyways, particularly in the trooping role. Many of these aircraft were fitted with Hercules 773 engines which could run on lower octane fuel than the original Hercules 763s, being designated as Hermes IVA.

Latterly the Hermes were flown on inclusive tour holiday flights from the UK. The last Hermes, G-ALDA, flown by Air Links Limited, was retired when it landed at Gatwick on 13 December 1964, and was scrapped nine days later.

Handley Page Hermes IV

Crew:	Seven
Capacity:	40-82 passengers
Length:	96ft 10in (29.52m)
Wingspan:	113ft (34.45m)
Height:	30ft (9.15m)
Empty weight:	55,350lb (25,159kg)
Max. take-off weight:	86,000lb (39,092kg)
Powerplant:	4 × Bristol Hercules 763 radial engines, 2,100hp each
Maximum speed:	350mph (567km/h)
Cruise speed:	270mph (437km/h) at 20,000ft
Range:	2,000 miles (3,242km) with 14,125lb (6,420kg) payload
Service ceiling:	24,500ft (7,470m)
Rate of climb:	1,030ft/min (314m/min)

Four 1,675 h.p. Bristol Hercules 10

A coloured supplement of the interior appeared in the April 5 issue of TH

SPAN	..	..	113 ft.	
LENGTH	..	..	80 ft. 6 ins.	
WING AREA (Gross)	..	1,408 sq. ft.	
HEIGHT, TAIL UP	..	31 ft.	
HEIGHT, TAIL DOWN	22 ft. 6 ins.	

ALL-UP WEIGHT	..	75,0
MAXIMUM LANDING		
WEIGHT	..	70,0
FUEL	..	..	2,57
OIL	..	..	120

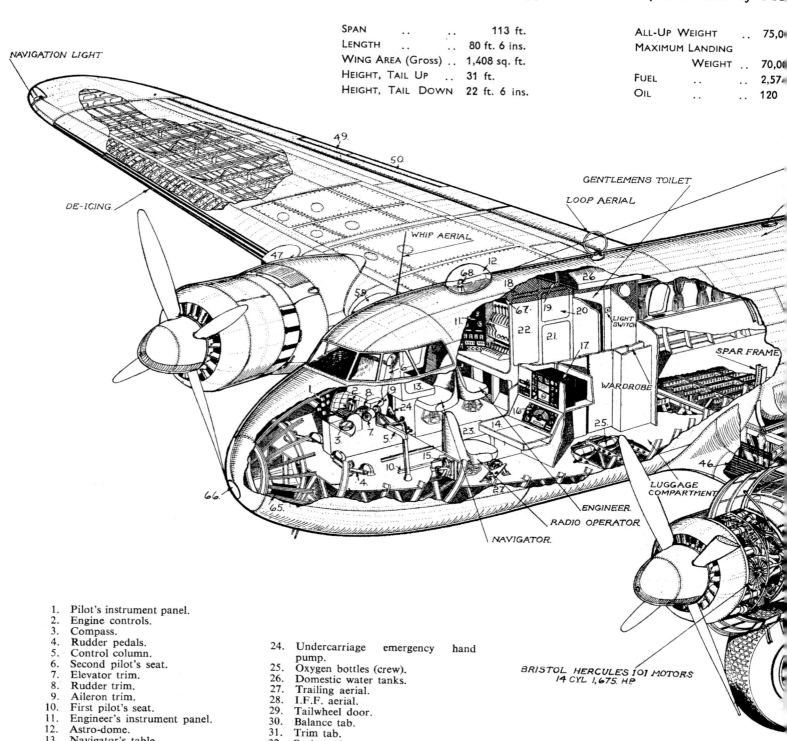

BRISTOL HERCULES 101 MOTORS
14 CYL 1,675 H.P.

1. Pilot's instrument panel.
2. Engine controls.
3. Compass.
4. Rudder pedals.
5. Control column.
6. Second pilot's seat.
7. Elevator trim.
8. Rudder trim.
9. Aileron trim.
10. First pilot's seat.
11. Engineer's instrument panel.
12. Astro-dome.
13. Navigator's table.
14. Radio operator's table.
15. Flying controls.
16. G.P. receiver.
17. G.P. transmitter.
18. Engineer's locker.
19. Astro-compass stowage.
20. Electrical bus-bar (behind).
21. Electrical auto-control generator panel.
22. Access panel to rear of Engineer's controls.
23. Crew entry and control access door.

24. Undercarriage emergency hand pump.
25. Oxygen bottles (crew).
26. Domestic water tanks.
27. Trailing aerial.
28. I.F.F. aerial.
29. Tailwheel door.
30. Balance tab.
31. Trim tab.
32. Spring tab.
33. Trim tab.
34. Aerial spring suspender.
35. Oil tank.
36. De-icing tank (port), similar tank fitted in starboard wing for airscrew de-icing, feeding four engines.
37. No. 1 fuel tank, 150 gal.
38. No. 2 fuel tank, 248 gal.
39. No. 3 fuel tank, 187 gal.
40. No. 4 fuel tank, 161 gal.
41. No. 5 fuel tank, 248 gal.
42. No. 6 fuel tank, 123 gal.

43. No. 7 fuel tank, 164 gal.
44. Oil tank, 43 gal. (max. capacity oil and air).
45. Undercarriage jacks, electro-hydraulic.
46. Engine controls.
47. Carburetter air intake.
48. Aileron.

49. Aileron t
50. Aileron s
51. Intermed
52. Centre w
53. Undercar
54. Escape h

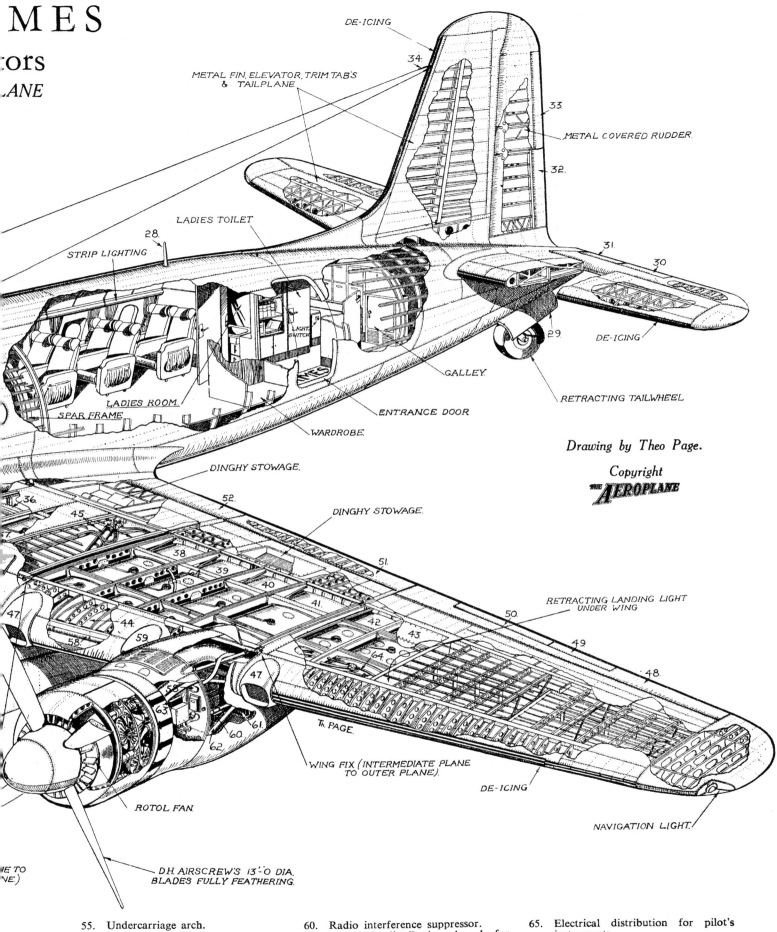

MES

ors

LANE

DE-ICING

34

METAL FIN, ELEVATOR, TRIM TAB'S
& TAILPLANE

33

METAL COVERED RUDDER.

32

LADIES TOILET

28

31

30

STRIP LIGHTING

DE-ICING

29

LADIES ROOM.

GALLEY.

SPAR FRAME

RETRACTING TAILWHEEL

ENTRANCE DOOR

WARDROBE.

Drawing by Theo Page.

Copyright

THE AEROPLANE

DINGHY STOWAGE.

36

DINGHY STOWAGE.

45

52

38

51

RETRACTING LANDING LIGHT
UNDER WING

39

47

40

50

41

49

44

42

59

43

48

58

64

47

WING FIX (INTERMEDIATE PLANE
TO OUTER PLANE.)

Th. PAGE.

DE-ICING

60

61

62

NAVIGATION LIGHT.

63

ROTOL FAN

D.H. AIRSCREW'S 13'·0 DIA.
BLADES FULLY FEATHERING.

55. Undercarriage arch.	60. Radio interference suppressor.
56. Lower radius rod.	61. Electrical distribution board for outer engine.
57. Hydraulic pump feeds to under-carriage jacks and brakes.	62. Engine mounting.
58. Heating system in wing for cabin.	63. Radio interference suppressor.
59. Cabin and oil cooler.	64. Fuel tank breather.

65. Electrical distribution for pilot's
instruments.
66. Taxi-ing light.
67. Main electrical control panel.
68. Sextant mounting.
69. Pressure-sealed electrical connections.

Airspeed Ambassador

The Airspeed AS57 Ambassador was a smart looking piston-engined design that was built specifically for BEA. Entering service in 1952, it proved popular with passengers, where the high wing layout gave them excellent views from the large windows. One of the first British airliners to be pressurised, sadly it will forever be remembered for the Munich Air Disaster which killed members of the Manchester United football team.

The Airspeed AS57 Ambassador was one of many British airliners to originate from the World War 2 Brabazon Commitee's consideration of what civil types would be needed when peace returned. Work on a prototype began in 1945 and the aircraft, G-AGUA, first flew on 10 July 1947, powered by two 2,600hp Bristol Centaurus 631 radial engines. The 28-50 seat aircraft had great passenger appeal, owing to its high wing design giving it a quiet cabin for its day.

A second prototype, G-AKRD, followed, with two static test beds and a pre-production machine, G-ALFR. This aircraft had the definitive Centaurus 661 engines and first flew in May 1950.

Twenty aircraft were built for British European Airways, the first of these flying in January 1951,

Right: Dan-Air was the last operator of the Ambassador and retired its final example in 1971. This airframe G-ALZO is the sole survivor of the production run of 23 Ambassadors and was delivered to BEA on 25 November 1952, who named it RMA Christopher Marlowe. In 1960 it was purchased by the Jordanian Air Force for use on VIP and transport flights, based at Amman. Three years later it was bought by Dan-Air (seen here) and was used to carry both passengers and freight. On 28 September 1971 it flew from Jersey to Gatwick, the last scheduled flight operated by an Ambassador, and was then retired to the Dan-Air maintenance base at Lasham. Today it is on display at Duxford.

Munich Air Disaster

In what became known as the Munich air disaster, an Ambassador crashed on take-off after a refuelling stop at Munich while operating a charter flight from Belgrade, Yugoslavia, to Manchester, England. This crash received tremendous public attention in the UK as it involved team members and staff of Manchester United Football Club, together with representatives of the national press. Tragically 23 of the 44 people on the aircraft died as a result of their injuries in the crash, including eight Manchester United players. The eventual enquiry decision centred on runway slush affecting the take-off speed adversely.

Left: The Airspeed Ambassador production prototype G-ALFR during a photo-sortie for the SBAC Show Farnborough in 1960, where it appeared as a Napier Eland engine test bed, but wearing BEA livery. After these trials it was converted back to Hercules power and was purchased and flown by Dan-Air until 1968 when it was scrapped at Lasham.

Airspeed AS57 Ambassador

Crew:	Three
Capacity:	Up to 60 passengers
Length:	82ft (24.99m)
Wingspan:	115ft (35.05m)
Height:	18ft 10in (5.74m)
Wing area:	1,200ft² (111.48m²)
Empty weight:	35,377lb (16,047kg)
Loaded weight:	52,500lb (23,814kg)
Powerplant:	2 × Bristol Centaurus 661 two-row sleeve-valve radial piston engine, 2,625hp each
Maximum speed:	312mph
Cruise speed:	260mph (418km/h)
Range:	550 miles (885km)
Rate of climb:	1,250ft/min (6.35m/s)

and the type entered service as the Elizabethan in March 1952. The first Elizabethan scheduled flight was from Heathrow to Paris Le Bourget on 13 March 1952 and the type later also served the key UK routes. By December 1955 the Elizabethans were each achieving over 2,000 flying hours annually, the highest rate in BEA's fleet. However, its days were numbered and the last Elizabethan service for BEA was operated in August 1958 before the type was replaced by the Vickers Viscount. The aircraft were passed on to other operators, including Butler Air Transport, The Royal Jordanian Air Force and Globe Air of Switzerland, BKS and Dan-Air.

The coming of turboprops and the dawning of the jet age caused the Ambassador to fall out of favour, sped up by the negative publicity arising from two fatal crashes.

Vickers Viscount

There are few civil aircraft that engender so much affection as the Vickers Viscount, the world's first turboprop airliner. Developed in tandem with the revolutionary Rolls-Royce's Dart engine, the Viscount became Britain's best-selling airliner with 445 built. Packed with cutting edge technology of the time, the Viscount was operated by both large and small airlines throughout the world, and was to remain in service for over 50 years.

The Viscount can trace its ancestry back to the end of World War 2 when the Ministry of Aircraft Production instructed Vickers to proceed with development of a 24-seater aircraft capable of transporting a payload of 7,500lb over a range of 700 miles at a cruising speed of 280mph at 20,000ft. During discussions with the Brabazon committee, Vickers advocated turboprop power. The committee was not convinced and split the specification into two types, the Type IIA using piston power, which led to the Airspeed Ambassador, and the turboprop-powered Type IIB, which Vickers was selected to develop in April 1945. Go-ahead was given in April 1945 for a 24-passenger pressurised aircraft powered by four Rolls-Royce Darts and two prototypes were ordered the following

Above: The Viscount 630 prototype G-AHRF was an unpressurised aircraft that first took to the air on 16 July 1948. It had the distinction of operating the first scheduled turboprop passenger service on 29 July 1950 in BEA livery from London (Northolt) to Paris (Le Bourget).

Left: When it entered service in 1953, the Vickers Viscount was ahead of its time and had no serious competitor. Little surprise that it achieved many international sales, including Turkish carrier Turk Hava Yollari (THY), featured here in this dramatic image.

March. British European Airways took a close interest and at its request the design capacity was increased to 32 passengers. Originally the airliner was named Viceroy, after the viceroy of India, Lord Louis Mountbatten, but the aircraft was renamed Viscount following India's independence in 1947. When construction began, official favour had switched to the Armstrong Siddeley Mamba but the Dart was back in vogue by the time the first prototype took to the air on 16 July 1948 as the Type 630, piloted by Joseph 'Mutt' Summers, Vickers' chief test pilot. Powered by early Dart engines, initial results of G-AHRF proved disappointing and at this stage the future of the aircraft was in doubt. The design was considered too small and slow at 275mph (443km/h), making the per passenger operating costs too high for regular service. However, the prospect of the vastly improved Dart 505 with 50 per cent more power gave Vickers the opportunity to offer a stretched version, the Viscount 700, with capacity for 40-53 passengers. In the meantime, G-AHRF received the first certificate or airworthiness for a turboprop airliner in July 1950, and passengers were immediately

Above :The first 'real' Viscount, the 700 prototype G-AMAV made its maiden flight on 28 August 1950, fitted with Rolls-Royce Dart RDa3 Mk504 engines. It was larger than G-AHRF with a 6ft 8in longer fuselage and 4ft 10in wider wingspan.

seduced by its smoothness, pressurised cockpit and large windows. Consequently, BEA ordered 20 Viscount 701s in August 1950, soon to be followed by Air France and Aer Lingus. The prototype V700 (G-AMAV) made its first flight from Weybridge in BEA colours on 28 August. Regular passenger flights were launched by BEA in April 1953, the world's first scheduled turboprop airline service. BEA became a large user of the Viscount and by mid-1958 its fleet had carried over 2.75 million passengers over 200,000 flight hours. Following BEA's launch of the type, multiple independent charter operators such as British Eagle were quick to adopt the Viscount into their fleets.

Much of the credit for the Viscount's subsequent success must lie with the Dart turboprop, its reliability, compactness, ease of access and quick development were key to the aircraft's attraction to the airlines.

Arguably the biggest 'break' in the Viscount's career came from an order by Trans-Canada Airways (now Air Canada) for 15 Viscount 724s, thus breaking into the lucrative North American market. Capital Airlines followed suit with an order for 60, the largest ever placed for a turbine airliner. Viscount 700Ds built to the Capital specification with Dart 510s became the most numerous version built with an impressive total of 150 manufactured.

The Type 810 introduced yet more powerful Darts and allowed higher weights. Production finally ended in 1964 with six for China.

The type continued in BEA and British Airways service until the 1980s, eventually being passed on to charter operators such as British Air Ferries (later British World).

On 18 April 1996, British World Airlines conducted the last Viscount passenger service in Britain, exactly 46 years after BEA's inaugural flight. Appropriately, on board the flight were two men instrumental in the record-breaking success of the Viscount, Sir George Edwards and Sir Peter Masefield.

The last British-owned Viscounts were sold in South Africa where a small number were the last in service, but these were retired by the early 21st century.

Below: Final assembly of the Vickers Viscount took place at both Weybridge and Bournemouth, before the aircraft were flown to Wisley airfield for fitting out. In 1953, the basic cost given for a Viscount was £235,000. By 1957, the Vickers production lines were producing the Viscount at a rate of one aircraft every three days.

Vickers Viscount 810

Crew:	Two pilots and cabin crew
Capacity:	75 passengers
Length:	85ft 8in (26.11m)
Wingspan:	93ft 8in (28.56m)
Height:	26ft 9in (8.15m)
Wing area:	963ft² (89m²)
Empty weight:	41,276lb (18,722kg)
Max. takeoff weight:	67,500lb (30,617kg)
Powerplant:	4 × Rolls-Royce Dart RDa.7/1 Mk 525 turboprop, 1,990shp each
Maximum speed:	352mph (566km/h)
Range:	1,380 miles (2,220km)
Service ceiling:	25,000ft (7,620m)

*Above: **The first lengthened Viscount was G-AOJA, a Series 802 built for BEA. It flew from Weybridge on 27 July 1956 and was delivered to the airline on Valentine's Day the following year. Sadly its career was to be short lived. On 23 October 1957, G-AOJA departed London for a flight to Belfast-Nutts Corner. At 16:45hrs the flight was taken over by the Precision Approach Controller for a GCA talkdown on runway 28. Within a mile from touchdown the aircraft had drifted right of the runway centreline. An overshoot was carried out, but the aircraft crashed 1,000ft south of the western end of runway 28. All seven occupants were killed.***

*Top right: **The well-designed cockpit of the Viscount was the first in a commercial airliner to feature instruments for jet pipe temperature (centre of the central consul).***

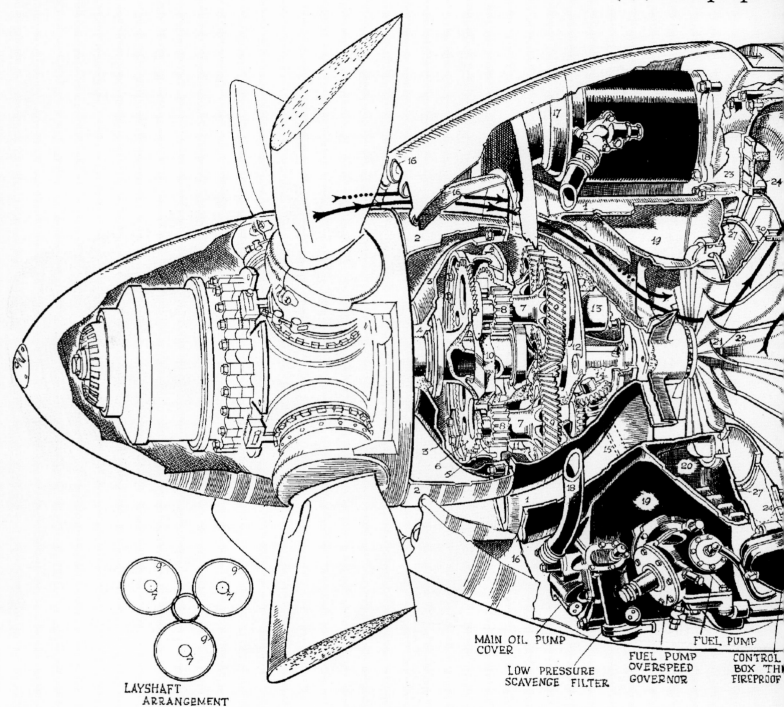

LAYSHAFT
ARRANGEMENT

MAIN OIL PUMP
COVER

LOW PRESSURE
SCAVENGE FILTER

FUEL PUMP
OVERSPEED
GOVERNOR

FUEL PUMP

CONTROL
BOX 'TH
FIREPROOF

1. Air intake casing.
2. Spinner extension.
3. Front reduction gearbox cover.
4. Airscrew shaft bearing.
5. Airscrew shaft annulus gear.
6. Airscrew shaft annulus coupling.
7. Layshaft.
8. Low-speed gear(s) (three used).
9. Helical high-speed gear(s).
10. Front panel.
11. Centre panel.
12. Rear panel carrier.
13. Torquemeter driven from No. 3 layshaft.
14. Drive to fuel and oil pump.
15. Shaft for 14.
16. Oil cooler air duct.
17. Oil cooler.
18. Oil cooler inlet pipe.

19. Oil tank.
20. Separate oil reservoir for airscr feathering.
21. Rotating guide vanes—made of steel
22. Light-alloy impeller.
23. Front compressor casing.
24. 1st-stage diffuser.
25. Turnover passage.
26. Inter-stage guide vane(s).
27. Low-pressure cooling air bleed.
28. Inter-stage guide vane casing.
29. Inter-stage bearing.
30. 1st-stage diffuser studs.
31. 2nd-stage rotating guide vanes.
32. 2nd-stage impeller.
33. 2nd-stage diffuser.
34. Intermediate compressor casing.
35. Top engine mounting.
36. Rear compressor casing.

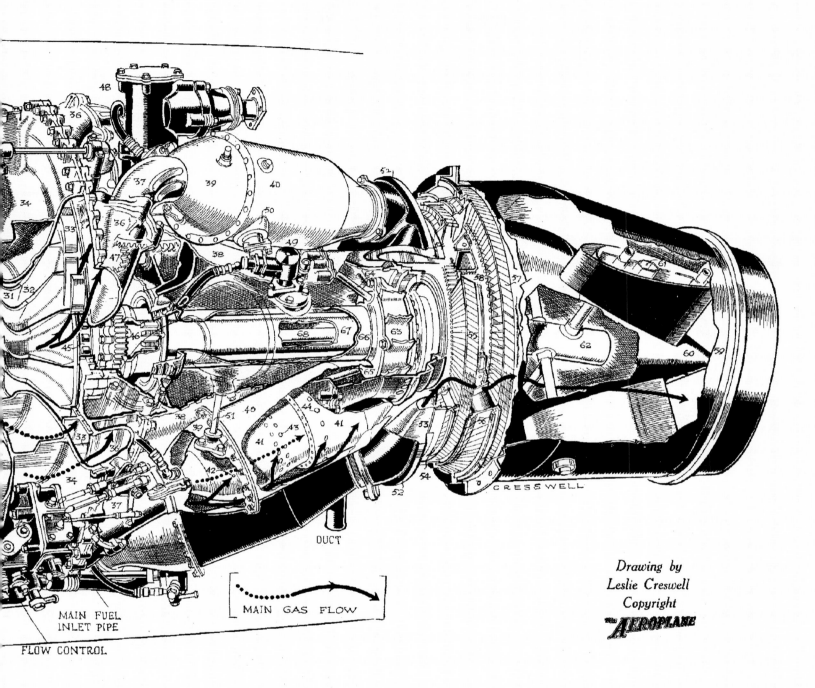

MAIN FUEL
INLET PIPE

MAIN GAS FLOW

FLOW CONTROL

DUCT

*Drawing by
Leslie Creswell
Copyright*
The AEROPLANE

. Compressor delivery elbows.	51. Drain tube (for surplus fuel when
. "Milk churn" conical backbone	starting).
member.	52. Nozzle box.
. Expansion chamber.	53. Discharge nozzle.
. Combustion chamber air casing.	54. H.P. stator guide vanes.
. Flame tube.	55. H.P. turbine blades.
. Primary air holes.	56. L.P. stator guide blades.
. Secondary air holes.	57. L.P. turbine blades.
. Tertiary air holes.	58. Inter-stage turbine seal.
. Centre bearing.	59. Exhaust cone.
. Coupling gear teeth, which also drive	60. Exhaust bullet.
auxiliary gear train.	61. L.P. cooling at rear stage turbine.
. Auxiliary gearbox gear-train.	62. L.P. cooling air duct.
. Auxiliary gearbox drive (50 h.p.—	63. Rear bearing assembly.
0.345 x engine speed).	64. Oil feed.
. Solenoid ignition assembly (No. 3 can	65. Scavenge oil feed from rear bearing.
is shown ghosted.)	66. Turbine shaft cover.
. Interconnector tubes.	67. Turbine shaft.
	68. Turbine assembly locking bolt.

Right: A night scene at Heathrow airport with Viscount 806 G-AOYL being turned round for its next flight. Delivered in early 1958, this aircraft was to end its days with British Air Ferries before being withdrawn from service in 1987 and scrapped in 1993.

Below: The comfortable and bright interior of a Viscount in the 1950s, with passengers demonstrating the fashions of the day. The lady's copy of Bloodstock annual 1951 is proving of irresistible reading to her fellow passenger.

*Above: **Capital Airlines of Washington was quick to embrace the revolutionary Viscount into its fleet and ordered 60 at a cost of $67 million. The Viscounts were deployed on the flagship Washington-Chicago route. N7402 was the first received by the US regional carrier and made its maiden flight from Bournemouth Hurn on 14 May 1955.***

*Below: **An early BEA Viscount service with satisfied customers disembarking G-AMOD. Passengers enjoyed the experience of flying in the new airliner, not least because of its smoothness and the views from its large oval windows. 'Oscar Delta' was first flown on 17 June 1953 and delivered new to BEA as RMA John Davis. It ended its days with VASP in Brazil before being withdrawn from service in 1969.***

Left: This advertisement from the early 1950s shows a Viscount in the colours of Air France overflying Paris. With a similar requirement to BEA, Air France ordered a fleet of 12 Viscounts for use on its European routes.

Below: Aer Lingus was an early customer for the Viscount and continued its association with the airliner to the extended Series 800, EI-AJJ being the second of the variant that it took on charge in 1958 and named St Columban. Here it is captured in suitably appropriate setting in front of the control tower and terminal of Dublin Airport. The aircraft was to remain with Aer Lingus for its complete service life before it was scrapped in May 1972.

Bristol Brabazon

The British airliner industry is littered with 'what might have beens', but they don't come any more grandiose than the Bristol Brabazon, the largest aircraft ever constructed in the UK. The prototype was completed and flown in 1949, only to prove a commercial failure when airlines felt the airliner was too elitist and too expensive to be useful. In the end only a single prototype was flown and it was ignominiously broken up in 1953 for scrap.

The Brabazon is synonymous with the Committee of that name that was formed during World War 2 to shape civil aviation in the UK once peace had returned to Europe. The committee's farsighted report urged the development of a large transatlantic airliner to secure the needs of postwar British commerce and industry. The primary requirement was for a large six/eight-engined airliner to fly non-stop across the North Atlantic, with a range of 5,000 miles at 275mph. In response, the Bristol Aircraft Company reworked a previously abandoned design for a long-range heavy bomber to produce the imposing Brabazon concept. In a remarkable demonstration of flawed thinking, the Brabazon Report assumed that the wealthy people flying in the aircraft would consider a long trip by air to be uncomfortable, so the specification called for luxury, demanding 200 cu ft of space for every passenger, and 270 cu ft for luxury class.

In November 1944, the design was finalised on what was to be the largest landplane then built, with a 177ft pressurised fuselage, 230ft wingspan, powered by eight Bristol Centaurus 18-cylinder radial engines mounted in pairs inside the wing. These eight engines would drive eight-paired contra-rotating propellers. Like many later aircraft, the Brabazon featured technologies such as electric engine controls, high-pressure hydraulics to operate the flying surfaces, and cabin pressurisation. A tremendous effort was put into saving weight. The Type 167 used a number of non-standard gauges of skinning in order to tailor every panel to the strength required, thereby saving several tons of metal. The large span and mounting of the engines close inboard, together with

Left: **The Bristol Brabazon was designed to carry more people faster, further, higher and in greater comfort than any aircraft that had flown before. Its most obvious feature was its size – at the time of its first flight it was the largest land-based aircraft in the world, dwarfing all other airliners. In this famous image, the aircraft is seen on final approach to Farnborough flying over the landmark Cody's tree.**

*Left: **Ambitious in concept and execution, the Bristol Brabazon was intended for luxury trans-Atlantic services that would be the envy of the world. In the event, the sole prototype, G-AGPW, only completed 164 flights before it was scrapped in October 1953.***

Bristol Brabazon MkI

Crew:	Six-12
Capacity:	100 passengers
Length:	177ft (54.0m)
Wingspan:	230ft (70m)
Height:	50ft (15m)
Empty weight:	145,100lb (65,820kg)
Max. takeoff weight:	290,000lb (130,000kg)
Powerplant:	8 × Bristol Centaurus radial engines, 2,650hp each
Maximum speed:	300mph (480km/h) at 25,000ft
Cruise speed:	250mph (400km/h) at 25,000ft
Range:	5,500 miles (8,900km) at 25,000ft
Service ceiling:	25,000ft (7,600m) at full weight
Rate of climb:	750ft/min (3.8m/s) at sea level

structural weight economies, demanded some new measures to prevent bending of wing surfaces in turbulence. The aircraft was initially designed to accommodate 80 passengers with sleeping berth accommodation, or 150 people for daytime flights, in considerable luxury. Proposed cabin layouts included provision for lounges, cocktail bars and cinemas. Although the prototype had old-fashioned piston engines, the turboprops on the anticipated production version would maintain a top speed of 330mph. This would allow a trans-Atlantic flight time of about 12 hours.

Building the aircraft was a challenge. Bristol's existing factory at Bristol Filton Airport was too small to handle what was one of the largest aircraft in the world, and the 2,000ft (610m) runway was too short to launch it.

Construction of the first prototype's fuselage started in October 1945 in an existing hangar while a gigantic hall for final assembly was built. Meanwhile, the runway was lengthened to 8,000ft (2,440m).

When the Brabazon was unveiled in December 1948, onlookers were astounded by its futuristic silver bullet appearance… it was sleek, it was luxurious, it was designed to rule the world. Optimism was high when it took to the air for the first time on 4 September 1949, captained by Bristol Chief Test Pilot Bill Pegg, who reportedly uttered the words 'Good God… it works!' Four days later, it was presented at the Society of British Aircraft Constructors' airshow at Farnborough before starting testing in earnest. Despite the general enthusiasm, BOAC never showed any

*Below: **The throaty roar of eight Centaurus engines echoes around Filton as the sleek Brabazon slowly begins its take-off role for another test flight. Despite its size, the Brabazon was considered an easy aircraft to fly with good handling characteristics.***

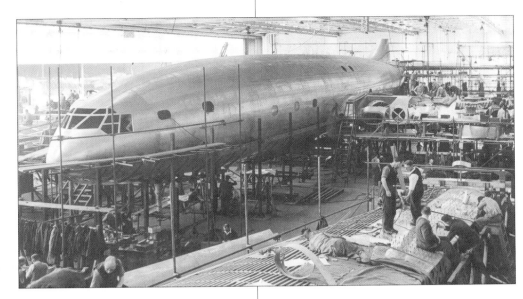

real interest in buying the Brabazon and the advent of turboprop engines during the aircraft's gestation period meant that passengers could now travel faster and above the bad weather, negating the need for excessive and uneconomical luxury. The second prototype never made it off the production line, and in 1953 the world's first and only Bristol Brabazon – the high-flying luxury liner of the future – was unceremoniously scrapped after just 164 flights, totalling 382 hours. The Brabazon project had cost £12 million to realise a reputed scrap value of just £10,000. It was to be another 20 years before the aviation world was to see the like of the Brabazon again, this time it came from across the Atlantic and was called the Boeing 747.

*Above left: **White elephant or ahead of its time? The bullet-like shape of the Brabazon fuselage disguised its large diameter, bigger than most wide-body airliners of today at 25ft (7.62m) and which would have featured a double-deck cabin.***

*Above right: **A view that truly emphasises the scale of the Brabazon fuselage, depicting the flight test instrumentation in the upper deck of the main uninsulated cabin.***

*Above: **The wingspan of the Brabazon was some 230ft (70.1m), more than that of a Boeing 747.***

*Below: **A sight to sadden the soul. The mighty Brabazon being cut up for scrap for a paltry £10,000, scant reward for £12 million of investment.***

De Havilland Heron

There was nothing fancy about the de Havilland DH114 Heron, but then that was the point. Essentially a scaled-up Dove with four-engines and a fixed undercarriage, it was more functional than a technological masterpiece, and that is exactly what appealed to its operators. The aircraft notched up nearly 150 sales the world over and examples were still flying into the 21st century, over 50 years after its maiden flight.

While the de Havilland Dove was proposed as a replacement for the company's Dragon Rapide, so the Heron was intended to replace the DH86 feederliner. The aircraft's design was based on the Dove, but with a lengthened fuselage for 17 passengers, and an increased wingspan to make room for two additional engines. It was of all-metal construction with fabric-covered control surfaces, and was laid out as a conventional design; the resulting aircraft was able to use many of the parts originally

designed for the Dove, thus simplifying logistics for airlines employing both types. The emphasis was on rugged simplicity in order to produce an economical aircraft for short-to-medium stage routes in isolated and remote areas that did not possess modern airports. A fixed tricycle landing gear eliminated the complications of a hydraulic system, and excellent short-field performance was assured by good wing design coupled with the use of variable-pitch propellers and unsupercharged Gipsy Queen

30 engines. The prototype G-ALZL was built at Hatfield and made its maiden flight on 10 May 1950 with Geoffrey Pike at the controls. The aircraft was unpainted at the time and after 100 hours of testing was introduced to the public on 8 September 1950 at the Farnborough Airshow, still glistening in its polished metal state. The first production Heron 1 was acquired by New Zealand National Airways in April 1952, this and all subsequent aircraft having a tailplane with considerable dihedral. The seventh production example (G-AMTS) served as the prototype for the Heron 2, incorporating retractable landing gear, which gave an increase in speed and a reduction in fuel consumption. Taking to the air on 14 December 1952, the Heron 2 replaced the earlier version on the production line, which was now established at de Havilland's Chester factory. The Heron 2 proved to be the most popular version, representing almost 70 per cent of the 149 Herons built. Despite these relatively small production figures, the Heron saw service in 30 countries, some with major airlines, many as luxury transports (including four operated by The Queen's Flight at RAF Benson), and about 25 of the total were used as communications aircraft by nine military services. The Heron was generally well-received by flight crews and passengers who appreciated the additional safety factor of the four engines. Performance throughout the Heron range was 'leisurely', and after production ceased in 1963, several companies, most notably Riley Aircraft Corporation, offered various Heron modification 'kits', mainly related to replacing the engines, which greatly enhanced take-off and top speed capabilities. Riley Aircraft replaced the Gipsy Queens with horizontally opposed Lycoming IO-540 engines. Production ceased in May 1961.

*Below: **Originally designed to follow on from the Dove, production of the Heron was delayed until there was a sufficient market. At a time when smaller airliners were still rare in isolated and remote regions, the DH114 Heron was able to provide reliable and comfortable service with seating for 17 passengers, in individual seats on either side of the aisle.***

THE DE HAVILLAND HERON

(Four 250 b.h.p. Gipsy Queen 30 engines)

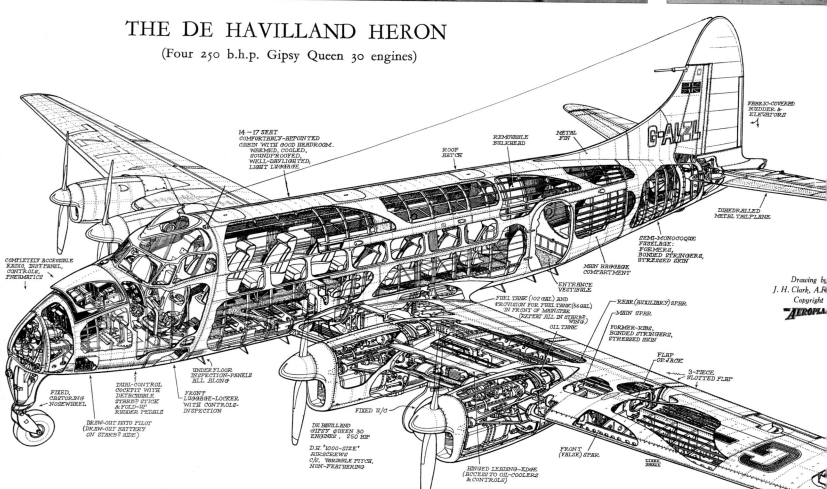

COMPLETELY ACCESSIBLE
RADIO, INST.PANEL,
CONTROLS,
PNEUMATICS

14—17 SEAT
COMFORTABLY-APPOINTED
CABIN WITH GOOD HEADROOM.
WARMED, COOLED,
SOUNDPROOFED,
WELL-DAYLIGHTED;
LIGHT LUGGAGE

ROOF
HATCH

REMOVABLE
BULKHEAD

METAL
FIN

FABRIC-COVERED
RUDDER &
ELEVATORS

DIHEDRALLED
METAL TAILPLANE

SEMI-MONOCOQUE
FUSELAGE:
FORMERS,
BONDED STRINGERS,
STRESSED SKIN

MAIN BAGGAGE
COMPARTMENT

ENTRANCE
VESTIBULE

FUEL TANK (102 GAL.) AND
PROVISION FOR FUEL TANK (56 GAL.)
IN FRONT OF MAINSPAR
(REPEAT ALL IN STARB?
WING)

OIL TANK

REAR (AUXILIARY) SPAR

MAIN SPAR

FORMER-RIBS,
BONDED STRINGERS,
STRESSED SKIN

FLAP
OP.JACK

3-PIECE
SLOTTED FLAP

FIXED,
CASTORING
NOSEWHEEL

DUAL-CONTROL
COCKPIT WITH
DETACHABLE
STARB? STICK
& FOLD-UP
RUDDER PEDALS

DREW-OUT AUTO PILOT
(DREW-OUT BATTERY
ON STARB? SIDE)

UNDER-FLOOR
INSPECTION-PANELS
ALL ALONG

FRONT
LUGGAGE-LOCKER
WITH CONTROLS-
INSPECTION

FIXED U/C

DE HAVILLAND
GIPSY QUEEN 30
ENGINES, 250 HP

D.H. "1000-SIZE"
AIRSCREWS
c/s, VARIABLE PITCH,
NON-FEATHERING

HINGED LEADING-EDGE
(ACCESS TO OIL-COOLERS
& CONTROLS)

FRONT
(FALSE) SPAR

Drawing by
J. H. Clark, A.R.
Copyright
AEROPLA

*Far left: **The de Havilland Heron prototype, G-ALZL, gleaming in its bare-metal finish during an early test flight. After achieving the type's certificate of airworthiness, this aircraft had a varied career flying with airlines in the UK and Denmark before ending its life transporting mine workers in Australia. It was retired in May 1976.***

*Left: **This could be all yours if you had £60,000 to spend in 1960. The Heron was popular as a luxury transport, as represented by this smart Series 2 that was operated by Shell Aviation as G-AOGC. In later life it was registered N572PR with Puerto Rico International Airlines in 1983. It was eventually scrapped.***

*Bottom: **Braathens in Norway were one of the first operators of the Heron and placed them into service in August 1952. The rugged basic aircraft proved ideal for operations in the sometimes harsh conditions of Scandinavia.***

DH Heron 2

Crew:	Two (pilot and co-pilot)
Capacity:	14 passengers
Length:	48ft 6in (14.79m)
Wingspan:	71ft 6in (21.80m)
Height:	15ft 7in (4.75m)
Empty weight:	8,150lb (3,705kg)
Max. take-off weight:	13,500lb (6,136kg)
Powerplant:	4 × de Havilland Gipsy Queen 30 Mk.2 6-cylinder inverted inline air-cooled piston engines, 250hp each
Cruise speed:	183mph (295km/h)
Range:	915 miles (1,473km)
Service ceiling:	18,500ft (5,600m)
Rate of climb:	1,140ft/min (5.8m/s)

Bristol Britannia

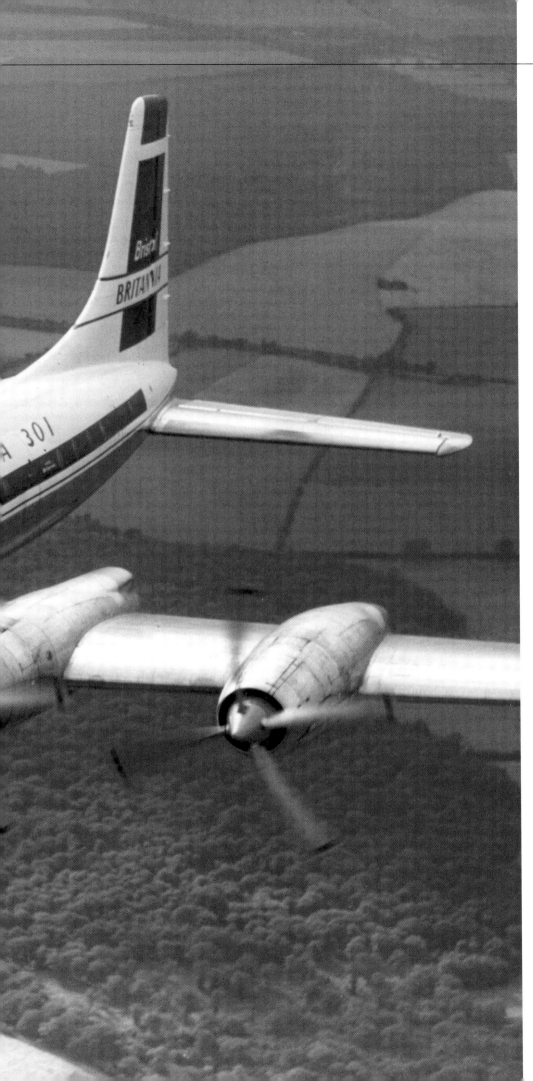

I f success were measured by aesthetics, then the majestic Bristol Britannia would have been a world-beater. Although considered by many as the ultimate turboprop-engined airliner, as a commercial project it must rank as an abject failure. Just 85 were built and the type's prolonged development saw it overhauled by jets before it had the chance to prove itself.

The 'whispering giant', as it was affectionately called, was a British medium-to-long-range airliner built by the Bristol Aeroplane Company in 1952 to fly across the British Empire. So closely was the type tailored to BOAC's needs that the result was to be an aircraft that had limited appeal to other airlines and was to hand the lion's share of the world airliner market to the far more commercially aware giants of Boeing and Douglas. The initial requirement was issued by the Ministry of Supply on behalf of BOAC for a medium range Empire airliner. Bristol designated the project Model 175 and go-ahead was given in July 1948, with three prototypes ordered as Mk 1 (powered by Centaurus piston-engine), with the second and third prototypes designated the Mk 2 (to be convertible to Bristol Proteus turboprops, then under development). BOAC finally signed up for 25 Bristol 175s in July 1949, the first six with

Left: The 'Whispering Giant' in all its stately glory. The Bristol Proteus turboprops were the first in the world to have 'control-by-wire' using the Ultra Throttle system. Sadly, the Proteus is mostly remembered for icing problems, which remained a 'continual potential hazard' that flight crews ultimately learned to manage with a 'high-lo' flight regime.

Bristol Britannia 310

Crew:	Four-seven
Capacity:	139 passengers (coach class)
Length:	124ft 3in (37.88m)
Wingspan:	142ft 3in (43.36m)
Height:	37ft 6in (11.43m)
Wing area:	2,075ft^2 (192.8m^2)
Empty weight:	86,400lb (38,500kg)
Max. take-off weight:	185,000lb (84,000kg)
Powerplant:	4 × Bristol Proteus 765 turboprops, 4,450shp each
Maximum speed:	397mph (639km/h)
Cruise speed:	357mph (575km/h) at 22,000ft (6,700m)
Range:	4,430 miles (7,129km)
Service ceiling:	24,000ft (7,300m)

the Centaurus engines and the rest with the Proteus, and now enlarged for 74 passengers. BOAC and Bristol eventually dropped the Centaurus plan entirely as the turboprop Proteus was showing such promise.

The name Britannia was chosen in April 1950 with Britannia 101 the designation for the first two prototypes powered by the early series Proteus 625. The first Britannia, registered G-ALBO, flew for the first time on 16 August 1952 at Filton Aerodrome with Bristol Chief Test Pilot A. J. 'Bill' Pegg at the controls. The maiden flight was eventful as the over-sensitive flying controls led to a wild pitching before Pegg restored level flight. The development of the Britannia 100 was delayed by a number of problems, including the loss of the second prototype (G-ALRX), which crash-landed on the shore of the River Severn in February 1954 following a severe engine fire. Continuing engine problems (related to icing issues),

delayed the Britannia's entry into service until 1 February 1957, about two years behind schedule. BOAC put its first Britannia 102s (now a 90-seater) into service on the London to South Africa route, with Australia following a month later. However, in the meantime Bristol had revised the design into a larger trans-Atlantic airliner for BOAC, resulting in the Series 200 and eventually the ultimate model, the 300 series, ordered by BOAC for its long haul services. This had a fuselage stretched by 10ft 3in (3.12m) and 45 were built. The main long-range version was the 312, of which BOAC took 18 and put them into service between London and

New York. The introduction of the Series 310 stimulated interest from El Al, Canadian Pacific and Cubana, which placed orders for this quiet, sophisticated long-range transport. But the age of the jet airliner was nigh…

BOAC withdrew its Britannias by the end of 1963 and many of its Series 100s ended up with the appropriately-named Britannia. Other operators took on the Series 310s, including British Eagle and Caledonian Airways. The Britannia saw out its days as a freighter operating throughout Africa and the Middle East. The last Britannia operations were with Katale Aero Transport of Zaire in the 1990s.

Below right: **The first Britannia 100 prototype (G-ALBO) in gleaming natural metal, makes engine runs in front of the famous Brabazon hangar at Bristol prior to making its maiden flight.**

Below: **In full BOAC livery, the first Britannia prototype graces the skies with its sleek beauty. After its early test flights, 'Bravo Oscar' continued to be used as an engine test bed until 30 November 1960, when it made its last flight to RAF St Athan where it became a maintenance airframe. It was broken up on 12 June 1968, having flown 1,794 hours over 692 flights.**

Below: **Owing to a catastrophic engine fire, Bristol's Chief Test Pilot Bill Pegg had to crash land the second Britannia prototype, G-ALRX, on a mudbank of the River Severn on 4 February 1954. All 13 occupants escaped without injury. The aircraft could not be rescued before it was covered by the rising tide and damaged beyond repair. The long and mucky process of dismantling the aircraft has already begun here.**

Above: **In a ceremony that promised so much for the future, Sir Reginald Verdon-Smith, right, Head of Bristol Aeroplane Company, hands over the first Bristol Britannia 100 to Sir Miles Thomas, Chairman of BOAC at London Airport.**

Top: **Britannia G-ANCA, the prototype of the extended Britannia 300. It made its first flight on 31 July 1956 but its career was tragically short lived. On 6 November 1957 it was returning to Filton after a test flight but at 1,500ft the right wing suddenly dropped and the aircraft went into a very steep bank and struck the ground in a wood near Downend. All 15 on board were killed. The cause of the accident has never been fully established, though a malfunction of the autopilot is suspected.**

Left: **The main instrument panel of the Bristol Britannia was laid out in an ergonomic manner consistent with modern airliners of the day.**

Above: **Bristol Britannia 300s in various stages of construction in one of the three bays of the giant Brabazon hangar at Filton. During the early 1950s, BOAC flew its Lockheed Constellations and Boeing Stratocruisers into Filton to be serviced in what was then the largest hangar in the world. The Brabazon hangar was also to gain fame as the birthplace of Concorde. Most Britannias were built by Bristol at Filton but 30 were constructed at Belfast by Short Brothers and Harland.**

Left: **Although not a mainstream success, Britannias were operated throughout the world. The 310 series (the Model 318) saw trans-Atlantic service with Cubana de Aviación starting in 1958 – despite the Cuban Revolution the airline had a special accord with British aircraft manufacturers to maintain this aircraft. Cubana de Aviación continued using various Britannias until March 1990.**

*Below: **Britannia and BOAC had high hopes for the Britannia, but the impending invasion of modern jetliners meant that scenes such as this were relatively short-lived. The Series 310 in the foreground, G-AOVB, had a particularly eventful career. First flown on 5 July 1957, it was purchased from BOAC by British Eagle International Airlines on 15 October 1963, but two years later was badly damaged after a heavy landing at Gan in the Maldive Islands. It was repaired and was later sold to Aerotransportes Entre Rios as LV-PNJ on 3 October 1969. It was converted to a series 312F, but was damaged beyond repair during a landing at Buenos Aires on 12 July 1970. The aircraft behind it, Britannia 102 G-ANBB, had an even more tragic tale. On 1 September 1966, it was being operated by Britannia Airways on a scheduled passenger flight from London Luton Airport to Ljubljana Jože Pučnik Airport (known as Brnik Airport at that time). During approach under cloudy conditions, the aircraft struck trees in the woods near Lahovče. Ninety-eight of the 117 passengers and crew died in the crash. The reason cited for the accident was a wrong setting of the altimeter.***

Military service

The Britannia was the RAF's first strategic airlifter when the first of 23 entered service in 1959, with Nos 99 and 511 Squadrons at RAF Lyneham. A crucial component in the reshaping of Britain's armed forces to meet the new threats of the Cold War, its tasks included the rapid deployment, worldwide, of the then newly formed Army Strategic Reserve, and supporting the V-Bomber Force. As a long-range military transport it could lift 18.5 tons over 4,000+ miles, carrying freight, or up to 53 stretchers with medical personnel and life support equipment or 115 passengers, in any combination. The Britannia was withdrawn from service in 1975.

Saunders-Roe Princess

Regal, majestic, magnificent. No matter how many adjectives you throw at the Saunders-Roe SR45 Princess, they never seem to do it justice. In the early 1950s, it was the largest flying boat ever built in Britain and, indeed, one of the largest aircraft ever conceived. It was designed to rule the skies… yet it was doomed from the start, finding no buyers despite its extraordinary capabilities. Caught at the crux of change, it was the pinnacle of flying boat designs launched into the dawn of the new land-based jet age.

The development of the Princess began in 1945 when Saunders-Roe was asked by the British Ministry of Supply to bid for a long-range civil flying boat for British Overseas Airways

Corporation (BOAC), which planned to use them on trans-Atlantic passenger services. The resulting proposal was on a grand scale and featured an all-metal flying boat powered by no less than 10 Bristol Proteus turboprop engines, powering six propellers. The four inner propellers were double, contra-rotating driven by a twin version of the Proteus. The two outer propellers were single and powered by single engines. The rounded, bulbous, 'double-bubble' pressurised fuselage contained two passenger decks, with room for 105 passengers in great comfort, an unprecedented load for its time. The planing bottom of the hull had only a slight step in the keel to minimise drag and retractable wingtip floats assisted in attaining a cruise speed of 360mph. Three prototypes were

ordered in 1946 with delivery planned to BOAC in March 1951, but delays to the powerplant meant that the first fully-functioning coupled Proteus was only received at the end of August 1951. By this time BOAC had re-evaluated its needs and determined it had no need for the Princess as it was planning to introduce the Comet on its international routes. The flying boat era had ended even before the Princess had got water under its keel. Nevertheless it was announced that construction of the three aircraft would continue as transport aircraft for the RAF. There was no denying that the Princess was an engineering miracle and the very size of the machine also proved a challenge to the manufacturer. The three Princesses were constructed in the large hangars at Cowes on

Above: **What an impression the Princess must have created on the crowds at Farnborough in 1953. Although an awe-inspiring sight (and sound), the reality was that the flying boat was already doomed and this was the swansong of a much-loved form of transport.**

the Isle of Wight. Even then, the planes were so huge that they had to be winched down to ensure that the 54ft high tail cleared the hangar doors. Only when the prototype Princess was outside of the hangar could the engines be fitted, along with the outer wings. Meanwhile, the cost of the project had risen from the original contract price of £2.8 million to £10.8 million and engine costs by tenfold to almost £5 million. Accordingly, in the spring of 1951 Saunders-Roe was ordered to suspend work on

the second and third machines and it was never restarted.

On 22 August 1952, the Princess prototype G-ALUN was taken out to sea by the company test pilot, Geoffrey Tyson. Once motoring around on the light waves off the Solent, Tyson reported that the conditions were perfect for a test flight and the Princess took to the air for the first time. After landing, Geoffrey Tyson described the Princess as handling like a fighter plane, not like a huge airliner at all and was stable, light on the controls and had an abundance of power. After its maiden flight, the prototype returned to the carefully outlined test programme and was soon issued a type certificate. In 1953, the Princess was displayed at the Farnborough Airshow in an attempt

to drum up business, but to no avail. Despite the best efforts of the marketing team, the projected high operating costs of the Princess drove off the few buyers who might have been enticed to consider the giant flying boat. Put simply, 10 engines and a huge hull that had to be constantly maintained against salt water corrosion, carried a huge cost. This glorious aircraft that astounded all who saw it, was indeed the proverbial flying white elephant. After 46 test flights and 98 hours of flying time, the prototype was grounded, never to fly again. The three aircraft were cocooned, one at Cowes and two at Calshot Spit, with the hope that work would be restarted if a buyer could be found. Despite various schemes, this did not materialise and they were broken up in 1967.

Right: **With barely an inch to spare, Princess flying boats are constructed in the Saunders-Roe hangars at Cowes, Isle of Wight. Some idea as to the scale of these aircraft can be gained from the workers who are dwarfed by the gargantuan dimensions of the machines.**

Far right: **Even in its moment of triumph, the Princess was a dinosaur from another age… but there can be few finer sights in aviation than this.**

Below left: **As you would expect for an aircraft of its size, the Princess' cockpit was spacious and neat… more than can be said for the flight engineer's panel that was festooned with gauges from 10 engines.**

Below right: **The Princess prototype G-ALUN is gently eased down the slipway at Cowes into the water on 19 August 1952. This view clearly illustrates the 10 Bristol Proteus engine installation, with four coupled pairs and singles outboard.**

Above: **If only… the sight of a Princess flying boat serenely cruising over the Sydney harbour bridge could only be created by the artist's brush.**

Saunders-Roe Princess

Crew:	Two pilots, two flight engineers, radio operator and navigator
Capacity:	105 passengers in tourist and first class cabins/137,000lb (62,142.2kg) disposable load
Length:	148ft (45m)
Wingspan:	219ft 6in (66.90m) with wingtip floats retracted. 209ft 6in (63.86m) floats extended
Height:	55ft 9in (16.99m)
Wing area:	5,019ft^2 (466.3m^2)
Empty weight:	190,000lb (86,183kg)
Gross weight:	330,000lb (149,685kg)
Max take-off weight:	345,025lb (156,501kg)
Powerplant:	4 × Bristol Coupled-Proteus 610 turboprop engines of 2,500hp each, plus 2 x Proteus 610s
Propellers:	4-bladed de Havilland constant speed, quick-feathering Duralumin propellers
Maximum speed:	380mph (611km/h) at 37,000ft (11,000m)
Cruise speed:	360mph (579km/h) at 32,500ft (9,900m)
Range:	5,720 miles (9,205km)
Endurance:	15 hours
Service ceiling:	39,000ft (11,887m)
Rate of climb:	1,900ft/min (9.7m/s) at sea level

Scottish Aviation Twin Pioneer

Twin Pioneer CC2

Crew:	Two (pilot and co-pilot)
Capacity:	Up to 13 troops or 2,000lb (907kg) of cargo
Length:	45ft 3in (13.79m)
Wingspan:	76ft 6in (23.32m)
Height:	12ft 3in (3.73m)
Wing area:	670ft (62m.)
Empty weight:	10,062lb (4,564kg)
Loaded weight:	14,600lb (6,622kg)
Max. take-off weight:	14,600lb (6,622kg)
Powerplant:	2 × Alvis Leonides 531 radial engine, 640hp each
Maximum speed:	143kts (165mph)
Range:	791 miles (1,287km)
Service ceiling:	20,000ft (6,098m)
Rate of climb:	1,250ft/min (381m/min)

Starting at the smaller end of the Dakota replacement scale was the Scottish Aviation Twin Pioneer (or Twin Pin as it affectionately became known). Designed for both civil and military operators, its party trick was that it could operate from an area only 30m (99ft) by 275m (902ft), a remarkable Short Take off and Landing (STOL) capability that allowed it to take on the shortest strips in jungles or frozen lakes in the Alps. Sadly customer confidence was shaken by two crashes due to fatigue failure, by which time the STOL requirement had largely been negated by longer runways.

The Twin Pioneer was designed by Scottish Aviation Ltd as a twin-engined STOL (short take-off and landing) transport aircraft for both military and civil use. Powered by two Alvis Leonides 531 radial engines, the Twin Pioneer was a high-wing cabin monoplane with a triple fin and rudder assembly and fixed tailwheel undercarriage. Speed was not its main consideration, cruising at 140mph over 400 miles, its box-like fuselage capable of carrying 16 passengers. To provide the necessary STOL characteristics it was fitted with the same high lift devices as its single-engined Pioneer predecessor.

The prototype Twin Pioneer, registered G-ANTP, first flew at Prestwick Airport on 25 June 1955, with Scottish Aviation anticipating sales of over 200 (rather optimistically as it turned out). Flight trials confirmed that the aircraft had a very short landing run and the aircraft was displayed at the September 1955 Society of British Aircraft Constructors Show at Farnborough where it stunned spectators with landing runs of only 180ft. Three pre-production aircraft were built for trials, sales and demonstration. By the time

Above left: The Twin Pioneer prototype, G-ANTP, in company livery. Originally fitted with Alvis Leonides 503 radial engines, in November 1958 it was converted to a Series 3 with Leonides 531s. It was written off after stalling on take-off at Jorhat, India, on 10 March 1960.

Left: Twin Pioneer production in full swing at Prestwick, with the type's distinctive triple tail fins being assembled in the foreground.

Far left: A local alternative to the Twin Pioneer, driven by a pair of grass-guzzling powerplants. The Twin Pioneer came into its own when engaged in operations from short airstrips and unprepared surfaces during the Borneo and South Arabian Campaigns of the 1960s and the Kuwait crisis of 1962. It was also successfully deployed on internal security duties in Kenya.

Overall: **This was how Scottish Aviation imagined the Twin Pioneer being utilised, in regions where air access was difficult. Here, second pre-production aircraft G-AOEO is seen being trialled by Swissair in January- March 1957 on service into airfields with restricted runways or frozen lakes, such as Davos, Zermatt, St Moritz and La-Chaux-de-Fonds. Due to the British registration it did not carry the Swiss cross, but the Swissair arrow instead on its tail. On 7 December 1957, while engaged on an African sales tour, G-AOEU crashed near Tripoli as a result of metal fatigue. Amongst the six killed was Grp Capt McIntyre, co-founder of the firm.**

Far left: **Only a small number of Twin Pioneers were actually used as airliners. In Britain the only airline to use the type was JFA of Portsmouth which operated services to the Channel Islands in the 1970s.**

Left: **The Twin Pioneer doing what it did best… showing its disregard for a conventional runway.**

production ceased in 1962, 87 Twin Pioneers had been built, finding their way into civilian and military service and operating in most continents of the world.

The rugged capabilities of the Twin pioneer appealed to the RAF, which eventually ordered 39, which were built between 1958-59. Deployed in Aden and the Far East, it was used extensively by British forces in the Malayan Emergency and the later confrontation in Borneo. The SRCU (Short Range Conversion Unit) at RAF Odiham also flew three Twin Pioneers for aircrew training. One Twin Pioneer also served as a STOL training aircraft with the Empire Test Pilot School (ETPS) at RAE Farnborough for many years.

Although mainly used in military operations, the Twin Pioneer was also successful as a commercial transport for operation in areas without proper airfields, where unprepared surfaces were often the norm.

Twin Pioneers were sold as survey aircraft to oil exploration companies with some of the first sales to Rio Tinto Finance and Exploration Limited, and the Austrian and Swiss government survey departments.

Handley Page Herald

The Handley Page Herald was one of several types developed in the 1950s as a replacement for the Douglas DC-3 short-range airliner, but unlike rival types such as the Fokker F27 and Avro 748, it was a commercial failure and in the event only 50 were built.

During its early efforts to find a market for its Marathons in the early 1950s, Handley Page established that there was a requirement for a similar layout but larger aircraft. The design that emerged was originally known as the HPR3 Herald and was an extensive re-development of the original concept of the Marathon, notable for its high mounted wing. The HP Reading division succeeded in producing a modern design with excellent flight and performance characteristics. However, the company made a

serious misjudgement and powered its aircraft with four Alvis Leonides piston engines, under the premise that airlines were still wary of the new turboprops. This was to be a costly mistake that meant that the promising aircraft lost ground to its turboprop-powered rivals.

Handley Page built two prototypes of the Herald as a private venture at Woodley, with the first G-AODE making its maiden flight from Radlett on 25 August 1955. At this stage, the design showed much promise and the Herald amassed a respectable number of 29 provisional orders. But the prospect of substantial further orders evaporated as airlines began to favour the promise of performance offered by the new turboprop engines. A second piston-engined prototype G-AODF flew in 1956, but following the worldwide success

of Viscounts and its arch rival the Fokker Friendship, Handley Page belatedly realised that turboprops were the way forward and converted the two prototypes to twin Rolls-Royce Dart power. Ironically, on 10 August 1958, the prototype Dart Herald was due to appear at Farnborough air show but suffered an engine failure en route from Woodley. The fuel lines ruptured and a serious fire ensued. The engine bearers burned through and the pilot, Hedley Hazelden, was forced to make a crash landing in a field. The landing was acknowledged as an astonishing feat of airmanship, but G-AODE was written off, striking yet another blow to the troubled programme. Fortunately G-AODF's conversion was nearly completed and it took over the flight testing.

The initial Dart-powered Herald 100 now carried 44 passengers over 1,635 miles at 275mph, and in June 1959 it received its first order from British European Airways for a lease of three aircraft for use on the carrier's Scottish Highlands and Islands routes. The Herald, had by this time, lost

Below: **The second Herald 100 prototype, G-AODF, equipped with a pair of Rolls-Royce Dart engines. In a bid to drive Herald sales, between April and December 1959 G-AODF made three sales tours resplendent in BEA livery, visiting 44 countries including an appearance at the SBAC Show at Farnborough. BEA used three leased Heralds on its Scottish islands routes.**

Left: **The Handley Page HPR3 Herald prototype was originally powered by four Alvis Leonides piston engines, but this was to prove a costly mistake by Handley Page.**

Below left: **The second Herald prototype in its four-engined guise. This aircraft made its maiden flight on 14 August 1956, but just over two years later was converted to Darts. In the winter of 1960 it was converted into the Series 200 prototype and was later re-registered G-ARTC. In competition against the Avro 748 it carried out rough-field trials at Martlesham Heath in February 1962 for the RAF military transport contract, but lost out to its rival. This aircraft was withdrawn from use in May 1962 and was scrapped at Radlett in 1969.**

its initial lead over the Friendship, which had entered service over six months previously. To stimulate demand, Handley Page launched a further improved version, the Series 200, which was lengthened by 42in (107cm), with corresponding increased weights, allowing up to 56 passengers to be carried, which attracted an order for six aircraft from Jersey Airlines. Basic price per airframe in 1960 was around £185,000. Jersey Airlines began operations with a leased Series 100 on 16 May 1961, receiving the first of its own Series 200s in January 1962, while BEA began Herald operations in March 1962.

The Herald attracted much early interest around the world because of its astonishing short-field performance and excellent flight

characteristics, but Handley Page failed to close many of the deals, losing out to the more popular F-27 and the HS 748.

One hope of improving sales was to develop the Herald as a military transport. The Royal Air Force had a requirement for 45 tactical transports to replace piston-engined Vickers Valettas, and Handley Page began work in 1960 on the HP.124 to meet this need. In early 1962 trials took place at RAF Martlesham Heath, but the contract was won by Hawker Siddely with a version of the HS 748, dubbed the Andover. Reportedly the short-field performance of the Herald put it in a very strong position to win the contract, but Handley Page's refusal to agree to a merger with the British Aircraft Corporation or Hawker Siddeley as part of the government's policy of consolidation of the British aircraft industry, scuppered the deal.

The later Herald Series 400 was a simpler tactical transport with a strengthened cabin floor and side loading doors that could be opened in flight for dropping of supplies or paratroops. Eight were built for the Royal Malaysian Air Force.

Meanwhile, by 1965, almost all sales momentum had been lost, and only 36

examples of the Series 200 production model were eventually built during the six years of production, together with the four Series 100s and eight Series 400s. The 50th, and last, Herald (a Series 200 for Israel's Arkia) was flown and delivered in August 1968, after which Herald production ceased.

On 17 March 1965, a Herald operated by Eastern Provincial Airways was flying from Halifax to Sydney when it suffered a structural failure and crashed near Upper Musquodoboit, Nova Scotia, killing all eight people on board. The fuselage had split lengthwise in mid-air along its belly owing to corrosion. After signs of more corrosion were found both in a British European Airways Herald and the Heralds operated by Alia, all Heralds in service were recalled by Handley Page for repair and corrosion-proofing.

In the end, the Herald made little impact as a Dakota replacement, but it did have some success with a number of second-tier airlines around the world. A number were later converted as freighters, with two operators in Britain being British Air Ferries and Channel Express, the latter taking the final Herald (G-BEYF) out of service in April 1999.

*Above: **The first production Herald 100 G-APWA first flew on 30 October 1959. Only four Series 100s were built before production was switched to the larger Series 200. 'Whisky Alpha' was originally leased to Jersey Airlines (here) before joining BEA to be based at Glasgow for the Highlands routes. The four 100s only remained with BEA until October 1966 when they were sold to Autair at Luton.***

*Top right: **A pair of Heralds destined for service around Europe. Nearest the camera is I-TIVE of Aerolinee Itavia. This HPR-7 Herald 203 was delivered in May 1963, but was written off during a landing accident at Rome Ciampino on 4 November 1970. During aircrew training, the instructor was simulating the loss of an engine during landing when the other engine actually lost power, resulting in a heavy landing. In the background is Herald 210 HB-AAG that was operated by the short-lived Swiss charter carrier Globe Air, based at Basel. Founded in 1958, its fleet initially comprised three Airspeed Ambassadors, but these were replaced by four Heralds, that were in turn supplanted by two Britannias.***

*Right: **In a bid to increase sales, Handley Page pitched the Herald against the HS 748 to provide the RAF's next medium transport. Company politics were to prove decisive in the failure of the Herald to win the contract.***

Handley Page Herald 200

Crew:	Two
Capacity:	56 passengers
Length:	75ft 6in (23.01m)
Wingspan:	94ft 9in (28.90m)
Height:	24ft (7.32m)
Empty weight:	24,960lb (11,345kg)
Max. take-off weight:	43,700lb (19,818kg)
Powerplant:	2 × Rolls-Royce Dart Mk527 turboprop, 1,910hp each
Cruise speed:	275mph (435km/h)
Range:	1,635 miles (2,632km)
Service ceiling:	29,700ft (8,140m)

Left: HPR-7 Herald 214 G-ASVO was delivered in 1964 and was a much-travelled aircraft having carried a total of 19 different airline colour schemes, including the likes of British Midland, Air UK, British Air Ferries and, finally, Channel Express. It joined the latter carrier in March 1992, but on 8 April 1997 it was taxied into a floodlight at Bournemouth International Airport and suffered extensive damage to its port wing. The aircraft was withdrawn from use and broken up.

Below: The Herald was another example of a British aircraft that 'might have been'. Had the correct engine configuration been made by Handley Page right from the start, the Herald might have defeated the Fokker F-27 to become a world-beating feederliner and the perfect DC-3 replacement that it was hoped to be.

Armstrong Whitworth Argosy

Originally designed to a military specification, the 'Whistling Wheelbarrow' – as the type was affectionately known by its crews – began its career as a commercial freighter, but was later adopted by the Royal Air Force, with which it served for 17 years as a valuable, if not exactly sparkling, performer. The last civil examples of the distinctive twin-boomer were still plying their trade in the USA until 1991, some three decades after the type's first flight.

In 1955 the British Air Ministry issued Operational Requirement 323 (OR323) for a medium-range freight- and passenger-carrying aircraft capable of lifting a load of up to 25,000lb (11,340kg) over a range of 2,000 miles (3,220km), which would fit in the RAF inventory between the twin-engined Vickers Valetta and the gargantuan Blackburn Beverley. Significantly, the specification also suggested that the type should be made attractive to potential commercial operators.

Accordingly, within six months Armstrong Whitworth had submitted a twin-engined design to the Air Ministry. The AW66 incorporated a high-set wing mounted to a truncated nacelle with a hinged 'beaver tail' provided with a loading ramp and 'air-doors' for dropping heavy loads by parachute. Two close-set booms extended from the rear of the fuselage, terminating in a pair of fins atop which was the tailplane, this arrangement being known as a 'pi-tail', as it resembled the Greek symbol.

Unfortunately for Armstrong Whitworth, by mid-1956 OR323 had been effectively abandoned, but having come this far the company decided to proceed with the design as a purely private venture aimed at commercial operators. The pi-tail and closely-spaced booms allowed little latitude in the design of the rear end of the fuselage, so the design underwent radical changes to become the AW650. Four Rolls-Royce Dart turboprop powerplants would replace the two engines specified in OR323, and widely-spaced twin booms offered ample clearance for the sideways-opening rear door. The biggest change, however, was the addition of a full-section sideways-opening door at the

*Left: **According to the dictionary, an argosy is 'a large merchant ship', and although the second of Armstrong Whitworth's commercial aircraft to bear the name was by no means the largest flying freighter in the world at the time, it nevertheless offered an attractive combination of a high volume of useable cargo space and flexibility for both commercial and military operators.***

*Below: **In a public demonstration of Armstrong Whitworth's confidence in its new design, it made the decision to bypass the usual process of constructing a single prototype and awaiting the results of its flight tests, and instead went ahead with the construction of production jigs, in which a complete batch of 10 aircraft would be completed, along with a pair of complete airframes for static and fatigue testing.***

Armstrong Whitworth AW660 Argosy C1

Crew:	Four
Span:	115ft (35.05m)
Overall length:	86ft 9in (26.44m)
Fuselage length:	64ft 7in (19.69m)
Height:	29ft 3in (8.92m)
Wing area:	1,458ft² (35.5m²)
Empty weight:	56,000lb (25,401kg)
Max take-off weight:	97,000lb (44,000kg)
Payload:	29,000lb (13,154kg)
Max cruising speed:	268mph at 20,000ft (430km/h at 6,100m)
Service ceiling:	23,000ft (7,010m)
Maximum range:	3,450 miles (5,550km)
Powerplant:	4 x 2,470shp Rolls-Royce Dart RDa.8 turboprop engines

front of the fuselage, an invaluable advantage for cargo operators, which could then load and unload freight from both ends of the aircraft simultaneously. This also provided a completely unobstructed cargo hold some 47ft (14.3m) long and 10ft (3m) wide at floor level, with a sill height of only 4ft (1.2m). The flight deck was repositioned in a bulged section high up on the nose above the freight compartment. Initially known as the A.W.650 Freightliner, the new aircraft was given the rather more poetic name Argosy in July 1958.

Investigations into the optimum wing for the new type led to the happy discovery that it already existed in the form of another product – the Avro Shackleton.

The new aircraft was to be more than just a freighter, an all-passenger variant was proposed, with seats for 83 passengers arranged six-abreast. A mixed passenger/cargo version was also envisioned, incorporating 36 passengers in six rows of seats, leaving 188ft² (17.5m²) of cargo space, the two sections to be divided by a removable bulkhead.

On 21 December 1958, the first Argosy, registered G-AOZZ, was rolled out of the Armstrong Whitworth factory at Bitteswell for engine runs and on 8 January 1959, the company's chief test pilot, Eric Franklin, took it aloft for its 62min trouble-free maiden flight. The distinctive new transport had been built and designed in record-setting time; 27 months from approval of the project to roll-out from the final assembly sheds. It was indeed a remarkable achievement. The new type showed such promise that before the first Argosy had

THE ARMSTRONG WHITWORTH A.W.65

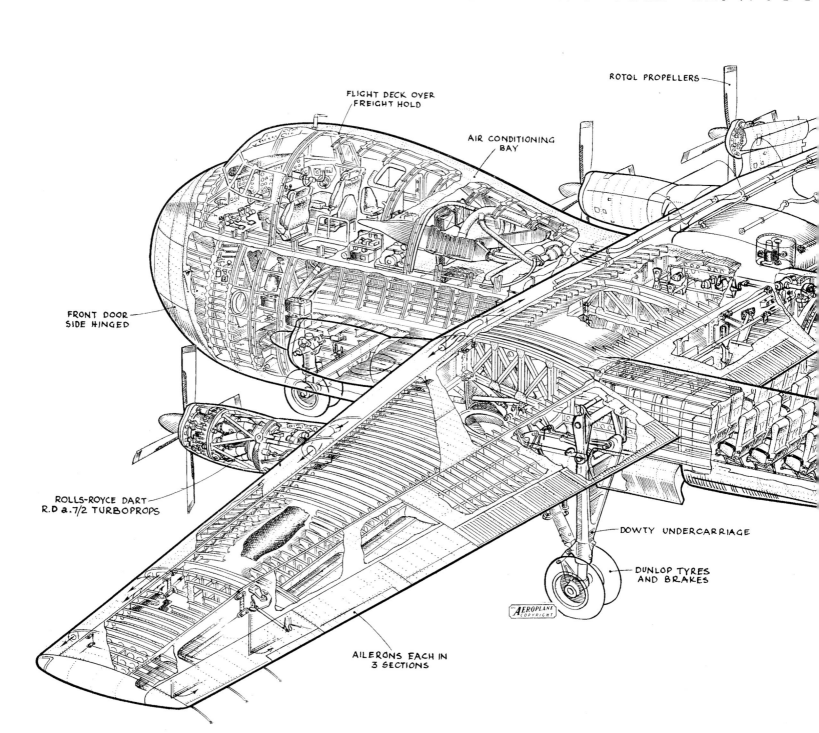

FLIGHT DECK OVER FREIGHT HOLD

ROTOL PROPELLERS

AIR CONDITIONING BAY

FRONT DOOR SIDE HINGED

ROLLS-ROYCE DART R.Da.7/2 TURBOPROPS

DOWTY UNDERCARRIAGE

DUNLOP TYRES AND BRAKES

AILERONS EACH IN 3 SECTIONS

flown, the Air Ministry had begun to show renewed interest in a military variant of the aircraft; there would be a place for the Argosy in the RAF inventory after all.

The Argosy Series 100 entered service with the American cargo airline Riddle Airlines, which purchased seven to provide logistics support to the USAF at the end of 1960. When Riddle lost the logistics contract in 1962, its Argosies were repossessed by Armstrong Whitworth and sold on to other airlines that had taken over the contracts from Riddle.

Meanwhile, BEA ordered Armstrong Whitworth's three remaining Series 100s as a stopgap until it could receive its definitive Series 220s, for which it placed an order for five in 1964. It lost two Series 220s in crashes and purchased another to replace the lost aircraft.

The small fleet of Argosies remained unprofitable, even when BEA received the more capable series 220s, and BEA withdrew its Argosy fleet in April 1970, replacing them with a freighter conversion of its Vickers Vanguard airliners.

Two aircraft were later operated by SAFE Air in New Zealand as the main link between the Chatham Islands and the mainland. Both aircraft were fitted with a pressurised passenger capsule. One of these aircraft was damaged beyond repair in a landing accident in April 1990, and a third Argosy was leased by SAFE Air from Mayne Nickless of Australia for five months during 1990 as a replacement.

The last of the Argosies, operated by American cargo airline Duncan Aviation, were withdrawn in 1991.

RGOSY

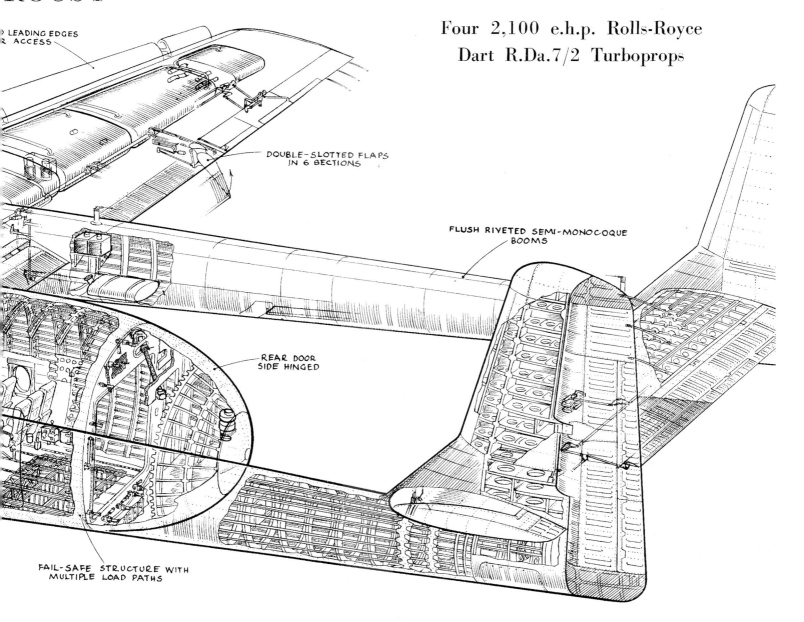

LEADING EDGES
ACCESS

DOUBLE-SLOTTED FLAPS
IN 6 SECTIONS

Four 2,100 e.h.p. Rolls-Royce
Dart R.Da.7/2 Turboprops

FLUSH RIVETED SEMI-MONOCOQUE
BOOMS

REAR DOOR
SIDE HINGED

FAIL-SAFE STRUCTURE WITH
MULTIPLE LOAD PATHS

Above: **Although the Argosy's wing was in a large part based on that of the Avro Shackleton, by the time the design had been finalised, 90 per cent of the drawings for the new transport's wing were brand new. Other economy measures involved using current production turboprop engines and nacelles from Vickers Viscounts, and making the twin booms out of sections of Gloster Meteor fuselage, since a nightfighter version of that jet was being built under contract by AW at the time.**

Left: **The first Argosy, registered G-AOZZ, was rolled out of the Armstrong Whitworth factory at Bitteswell on 21 December 1958 and made its maiden flight on 8 January 1959. Effectively a production aircraft in its own right, it ended up hauling military equipment for Universal Airline and Duncan Aviation in the USA as N896U. It logged its last flight time in September of 1990 and it is believed that this was one of the last flights for any Argosy.**

Top right: **US cargo operator Riddle Airlines was the first carrier to receive the Argosy using it on USAF contracts in 1960. Twenty years later, by the end of the 1980s, the 73 Argosys build by AW were rapidly dwindling. Their ranks had been thinned by lack of spare parts and the survivors were being replaced by more fuel efficient aircraft. Three are preserved in museums in the UK, three more in the US and one in New Zealand, however none remain airworthy.**

Loading the Argosy

Various schemes for loading the Argosy can be used, according to the needs of the operator. On the right are three layouts for freight and passenger accommodation. The other four sketches show a freight-loading system using a roller-floor and bridge or ramp for varying truck-bed heights. This system has been developed by Armstrong Whitworth for the Argosy, but others such as the Cargon system can be incorporated in the aircraft if required.

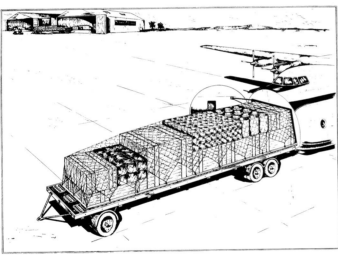

A loaded trailer with roller-floor at the same height as the Argosy floor allows very rapid loading of the freight hold, the loaded pallet being winched into the 3,680-cu. ft. hold.

Top, a pure freight layout with 426 sq. ft. of floor area.

Centre, a mixed freight and passenger layout.

Bottom, a 75-passenger version with toilet and galley services.

Man-handling of packing cases presents little difficulty when truck and aircraft both have roller-floors.

Left, a large case is manœuvred into position for winching into the Argosy hold.

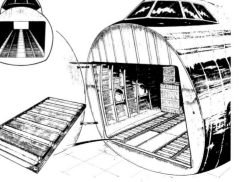

Right, the roller-floor can be easily removed and inverted to form a normal surface.

Above: **A true British classic, the unmistakable shape of the Armstrong Whitworh Argosy was always a popular sight. The two booms extending back from the fuselage, and the sound of the Rolls-Royce Dart turboprops, gave rise to the nickname, 'Whistling Wheelbarrow'.**

Left: **The small fleet of BEA Argosies did not prove to be profitable, and it withdrew its fleet in April 1970. The twin tail-boom configuration is well-shown here. Behind each inboard engine extended a strong light-alloy tubular structure that accommodated a main undercarriage unit and blended into the tailboom. Each boom was structurally identical with its partner and at the end of each was attached a small non-structural glass-fibre dorsal fin which connected to the fin stubs and carried mountings for the tailplane. The tailplane was made in one piece and incorporated two spars.**

Left: **The crew of the Argosy entered the aircraft through a hinged circular hatch in the underside of the nose, which led directly into the front of the hold. The flight deck could then be reached by climbing a retractable ladder. The civil variants normally operated with a crew of two, whereas standard crew for an RAF Argosy comprised two pilots, a navigator and a flight engineer. The flight deck and the hold were both pressurised.**

RAF Argosy C1

The Argosy was used by the Royal Air Force for its capability to accommodate 69 troops, 48 stretcher cases or 29,000lb (13,000kg) of freight. From the outset the military Argosy was to be fitted with 'clamshell' or 'crocodile-jaw' doors at the rear of the fuselage, in contrast to the starboard-hinging aft section of the civil freighter, in order to ease rapid vehicle loading and the air-dropping of heavy equipment on pallets. This meant it could carry military equipment such as the Saracen or Ferret armoured cars, or artillery such as the 105mm (4.13in) howitzer or Wombat.

The RAF eventually received 56 Argosies, the earliest deployments being in 1962 to No 105 Squadron in the Middle East and Nos 114 and 267 Squadrons at RAF Benson. The following year, No 215 Squadron received its Argosies when based at RAF Changi, Singapore. The squadron was disbanded on New Year's Eve 1967, and the aircraft went to No 70 Squadron at RAF Akrotiri, Cyprus. This was the last squadron to operate the aircraft in the transport role when it retired the last aircraft in February 1975. They ended their days as radar calibration aircraft, their four huge propellers providing excellent radar targets in the air.

*Above: **The RAF version (Argosy C1) added a 3ft diameter radome in the centre of the suggestively shaped nose, which caused crews to dub it 'The Whistling T*t'. The civil AW650's four Rolls-Royce Dart RDa.7 turboprop engines were replaced on the military AW660 with a quartet of 2,470shp Dart RDa.8s (Mk101s), each driving a Dowty-Rotol propeller of 11ft 6in (3.5m)-diameter. It was found, however, that performance with the Mk101 Darts was not as good as expected, and these were ultimately replaced in service with Dart Mk102s, which provided an improvement of more than 2,000ft (610m) in cruising altitude in poor weather conditions. The Argosies provided vital supplies to Commonwealth troops fighting in the jungles of Borneo during the Indonesian Confrontation of 1963–66***

*Below: **AW660 Argosy C1, XR106, No 114 Squadron, RAF, circa 1970.***

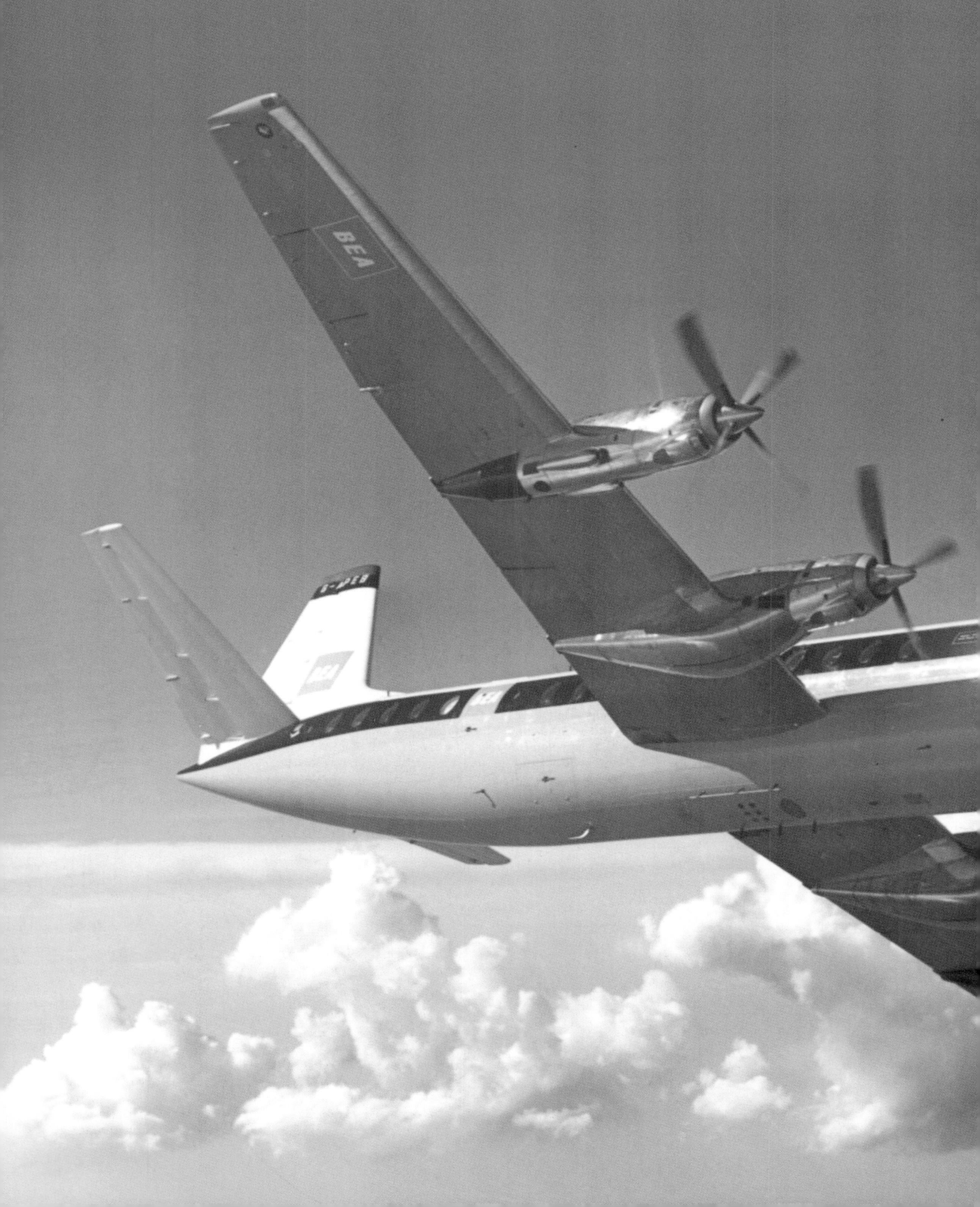
BEA
BEA

Vickers Vanguard

I t was always going to be a difficult task for Vickers to follow the success of the revolutionary and record-breaking Viscount, and so it proved with the Vanguard short/medium-range turboprop airliner introduced in 1959. Although the large turboprop never achieved the acclaim or success of its illustrious forebear, this could be attributed more to bad timing rather than bad design. The Vanguard was introduced just before the first of the large jet-powered airliners and was subsequently ignored by a market seduced by the new technology. Only 44 Vanguards were built and although its success as an airliner was relatively short-lived, in its Merchantman freighter guise, the design remained in service until 1996.

Top: **More sturdy than sleek, the Vanguard did not achieve the success that Vickers was hoping for, though it did have good performance and operating costs.**

Left: **As a second-generation turborpop airliner, the Vanguard benefitted from new Rolls-Royce Tyne powerplants that gave it a performance virtually comparable to the early jet airliners. However, the travelling public viewed anything with propellers as old-fashioned and its time as an airliner was short-lived, though it did carve out a relatively successful career as a cargo carrier.**

During the 1950s, Vickers worked on a variety of designs for a Viscount replacement, mainly driven by a requirement from BEA for a 100-seat turboprop. Designated the Type 870, the design also attracted interest from Trans-Canada Airlines, but it wanted an increased freight-carrying capability. Vickers proposed a revised Type 950 to fill both requirements, effectively a compromise to satisfy both airlines. Vickers started with the original Viscount fuselage, but cut it off about halfway up from the bottom, replacing the top section with a larger-diameter fuselage to give it a 'double bubble' cross-section (similar to the Boeing Stratocruiser). The result of the larger upper portion was a roomier interior, with increased cargo capacity below the floor. Finally emerging as the Vickers VC9 Vanguard, the airliner carried 139 economy passengers over 1,830 miles powered by four of the new 4,470hp Rolls-Royce Tyne turboprops. These new engines allowed for a much higher service ceiling and a cruising speed of 420mph, making the Vanguard one of the fastest turboprops ever built.

Otherwise, construction was entirely conventional except for the wing, which introduced integrally machined skins of light alloy to provide span-wise stiffening at low cost. The Vanguard featured a spacious passenger cabin with large windows and six-abreast

seating. BEA made a firm order for 20 aircraft in July 1956 (G-APEA-PEU) and this was shortly followed by what was thought to be the vital first North American order when TCA placed an order for another 20 (it eventually received 23), valued at £23.9 million.

The prototype Vanguard G-AOYW was rolled out at Weybridge on 4 December 1958 for ground testing. Following problems with the initial Rolls-Royce Tynes, G-AOYW made an 18min first flight from Weybridge to Vicker's Test Airfield at Wisley on 20 January 1959, piloted by Jock Bryce and Brian Trubshaw. During its flight trials the Vanguard experienced vibration and stalling problems and Brian Trubshaw later related that the aircraft carried out more than 2,000 stalls before an acceptable performance was achieved.

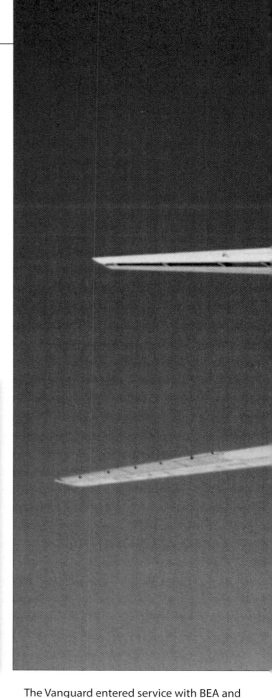

*Below: **The double-bubble design of the Vanguard's fuselage is clearly evident in this construction shot taken at Vicker's plant at Weybridge. The top part of the fuselage was based on the Viscount, while the latter section was designed to increase the aircraft's cargo-carrying capability.***

Vickers Vanguard

Crew:	Two-three
Capacity:	139 passengers
Length:	122ft 10in (37.50m)
Wingspan:	118ft 7in (36.10m)
Height:	34ft 11in (10.60m)
Wing area:	1,527ft² (142m²)
Empty weight:	82,500lb (37,421kg)
Loaded weight:	141,000lb (63,977kg)
Powerplant:	4 × Rolls-Royce Tyne Mk512 turboprop, 5,545hp (4,700 shp, 4,135 kW) each
Maximum speed:	425 mph (684 km/h)
Range:	1,830 miles (2,945km)
Service ceiling:	30,000ft (9,145m)

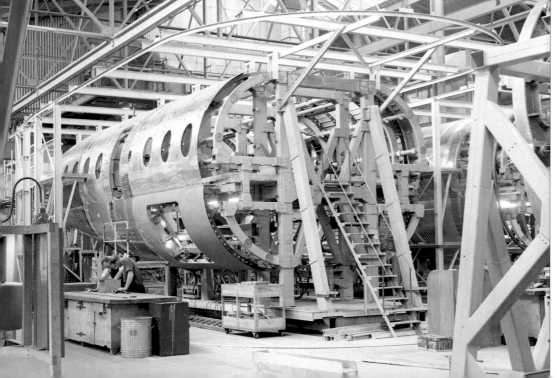

The Vanguard entered service with BEA and TCA in late 1960. BEA operated its first Vanguard schedule on 17 December from Heathrow to Paris. Following delivery of its full fleet of six V951 and 14 V953 aircraft by 30 March 1962, the type took over many of BEA's busier European and UK trunk routes. Initial seating was 18 first-class at the rear and 108 tourist, but this was changed to 139 all-tourist, in which configuration the Vanguard had very low operating costs per seat/mile. On flights up to 300 miles (480km), such as from London to Paris, Brussels and Amsterdam, the type could match the block times of the pure jets which were being introduced in the early 1960s. TCA initiated Vanguard schedules on 1 February 1961 with two flights from Toronto and Montreal via intermediate stops to Vancouver. The fleet was also used on services from Toronto and Montreal to New York and Nassau,

Bahamas. However, by then the Vanguard and other second-generation turboprop-powered airliners had been deposed by the development and introduction into service of economical turbojet-powered airliners such as the Boeing 707. With no other orders placed, the final Vanguard was delivered in November 1962, two years before the last Viscount was delivered! The remaining BEA fleet passed to British Airways on 1 April 1974 and the last BA passenger flight with the type was on 16 June 1974… but this was not the end of the story.

Back in 1969 TCA had experimentally converted one of its Vanguards to a freighter configuration by removing all its seats, calling it the Cargoliner, in which role it could carry 42,000lb (19,050kg) of freight. In the event, it was the only such TCA conversion, but it survived to be the last Canadian Vanguard to be retired in December 1972. However

*Above: **After construction at Vicker's plant in Weybridge, Vanguards were flown from the short Brooklands runway to nearby Wisley for flight testing and fitting out before delivery to customers.***

*Top: **The Vanguard could cruise at 30,000ft and was one of the fastest turboprops ever built with a top speed of 425mph. This aircraft is CF-TKB (c/n 9020) and was delivered to TCA on 14 December 1961. It ended its career with Air Holding Ltd.***

the experiment was largely considered to be successful and in the early 1970s most remaining BEA Vanguards were converted into freighters with a large forward cargo door, becoming the V953C Merchantman. These aircraft continued in service with BA until late 1979 when the remaining five were sold. Air Bridge Carriers purchased several of the Merchantman and operated them until 1992, when it changed to Hunting Cargo Airlines. Hunting Cargo operated its last V953C flight on 30 September 1996.

Left: **Airliner flying 1960's style was a very relaxed occasion, though the passengers at London (Heathrow) Airport were left exposed to the elements during winter.**

Right: **Passengers offload from a Vanguard in front of the control tower at Manchester Airport in the 1960s.**

Below left: **A pair of BEA Vanguards on the apron during a night turnaround at London (Heathrow) Airport. BEA anticipated that there would be a need for larger turboprops on medium/short-haul routes in the 1960s, failing to predict the appeal of the new jets amongst passengers.**

Below: **What better way to spend a Christmas Eve in the early 1960s than wrapping up in the latest fashion and visiting the public viewing area at London (Heathrow) Airport to watch Vanguard operations?**

Bottom: **With its windows blanked-out, the Merchantman was the freight-conversion of the Vanguard, which gave the aircraft a new lease of life following its withdrawal from scheduled passenger services.**

Vanguard casualties

The Vanguard did not have the best safety record and over its 36 year career, five were lost in accidents:

On 27 October 1965, BEA Vanguard G-APEE flying from Edinburgh Airport to London Heathrow Airport attempted an overshoot during a landing in poor visibility, but crashed on runway 28R. All six crew and 30 passengers on board died.

On 2 October 1971, BEA Flight 706 operated by Vanguard G-APEC crashed near Aarsele in Belgium. The cause was the failure of the rear pressure bulkhead and subsequent destruction of the tailplane. All eight crew and 55 passengers on board died.

On 10 April 1973, Invicta International Airlines Flight 435, operated by Vanguard G-AXOP crashed near Basel-Mulhouse Airport Switzerland. Four crew and 104 passengers on board died.

On 29 January 1988, Inter Cargo Service Flight 1004, operated by Merchantman F-GEJF, crashed at Toulouse-Blagnac Airport when take-off was attempted with only three fully operable engines. There were no casualties of the three crew and one passenger aboard.

On 6 February 1989, Inter Cargo Service Flight 3132, operated by Merchantman F-GEJE, crashed on take-off from Marseille-Marignane Airport, France. Three crew died.

Left: A number of Vanguards were lost during operations including G-APEC, pictured in the foreground here. En route from London to Salzburg at an altitude of 19,000ft the rear pressure bulkhead ruptured. An explosive decompression of the fuselage occurred, causing serious interior damage and severe distortion of the outer skin. The tail surfaces subsequently failed, causing the aircraft to enter a steep dive. The Vanguard spiralled down out of control and crashed in a field next to a highway killing all 63 on board.

During the investigation, corrosion was found in the lower part of the rear pressure bulkhead underneath plating that was bonded to the structure. Fluid contamination, perhaps from the lavatory, was thought to have been the root cause for the corrosion.

Freight operations by a number of second-tier carriers took the Merchantman to unusual climes with airlines in Iceland, Indonesia, France and Sweden, the latter pictured here.

KEY

Fuselage

1 Front pressure bulkhead
2 Wide side-entry to pilots' seats
3 Unpressurised nosewheel box
4 Passenger's entrance with power-folding airsteps
5 Emergency and galley service door (to starboard)
6 Galley and steward's seat
7 Forward cargo hold and large loading hatch near to ground with upper and lower half-doors, as (8)
9 Moveable bulkhead, standard position (9), alternative positions (10)
10 Alternative bulkhead positions
11 Two washrooms each side, or with wardrobes
12 Rear underfloor cargo hold with large loading hatch
13 Wardrobes, passengers' entrance door and airsteps
14 Galleys with emergency and galley service doors between
15 Angled doors to two washrooms
16 Rear pressure bulkhead forms back wall to washrooms
17 Emergency door and steward's seat
18 Six-across seating (thrift-class layout)
19 Five-across (tourist layout)
20 Four-across seating (first-class layout)
21 Seats have rail and side fixing
22 Typical structures (frames, proud stringers, stressed skin, with floor beams (23), side wall (24) to services compartment all along, and stressed floor (25) to hold
26 Built-in three-web centre section with lugs as (27)
28 Inspection manholes
29 Three-web fin and tailplanes, with fixings

Wings

30 Butt-joints and straps (centre section to inner wing)
31 Solid-wall rib (end of fuel tankage)
32 Top-skin manholes
33 Bracketing for engine pick-ups
34 Four-plank skinning with integral stiffners
35 Butt and strap joint (inner to outer wing)

36 Solid-wall rib (barrier between inner and outer fuel tanks)
37 Plated inspection cut-outs in front and rear spars
38 Aileron inspection panels all along, below and above
39 End of inner wing trailing section
40 End of outer wing middle spar
41 Three-plank skinning
42 Fuel tankage right out to wingtip
43 Fuel jettison pipe

Flying controls (elevator, rudder and aileron)

44 From stick (44) with its parallel motion strut (45) to elevator via hinge-point (46), links (47) and rods along services compartment (as at 24), then under centreplane and aft to gland-box (48) and gaiter (49)
50 Floor cut away to reveal gland-box mounted on fuselage skin free of pressure bulkhead (16) to allow for difference in expansion of fuselage and controls
51 Cut-out in (16) reveals control rods (52) to tail from (48). The rods pass clear through (16) with (49) as seal
52A Rudder and elevator auto-pilot servo motors
52B Geared (auto) tab
52C Spring (hand) tab
53 Rudder pedals in fore-and-aft tracks, linkages, 54, 55, 56, thence along and under wing to (48) and (52)
57 From stick (44) and linkage (57) along fuselage and under centre section to aileron rods (58) at rear spar, linkage (59) to spring tab (60)
61 Hand trim linkage
62 Geared (auto) tabs
63 Aileron servo (in centre section)

Flying controls (flaps)

64 Flap guide-rail outrigger
65 Flap guide-and-tilt rail outrigger (straight top rail carries pair of flaps, curved lower rail tilts flaps)
66 Hydraulically-operated screwjack behind starboard back-spar rotates operating rod (67) to pull flaps in and out

Undercarriage

68 Main pick-up of forwards-retracting main undercarriage
69 Radius-rod pick-up
70 Operating jack
71 Main pick-ups of forwards-retracting nosewheel leg (carries steering jack 72)
73 Radius-rod pick-up, door retraction and UP-latch beam
74 Oleo-positioning track and wheel brake

Engine installations

75 Tyne engine inlet casing
76 Gearcase with power-take-off to auxiliaries' gearbox (77)
77 All four gearboxes carry on the front face a breather, propeller parking-brake pump, hydraulics system pumps, and alternator. Outer two gearboxes carry alternator on back face. The inner gearboxes carry blower on back
78 Rubber mounting blocks (in bearer feet on engine)
79 Combustion chambers and turbine section
80 Engine fireproof bulkhead. Engine exhaust unit protrudes into jet pipe exhaust cone attached to (81)
81 Second fireproof bulkhead carrying engine snubber ring and exhaust cone
82 Jet pipe
83 Oil cooler and airflow (84)

Engine ventilation and fire protection

85 Zone 1 (from front back to 80) air bled off 84 and in via 86. Out at 87
85A Zone 1A
88 Zone 2 (entry at 89)
90 Zone 3 (on inboard it is fed from cowling intake, but on outboard it is fed off heat-exchanger ram air)
91 Zone 3A with inlet and outlet (92)
93 Two groups of two bottles in each wing. Each group serves its own nacelle and the other nacelle
94 Spray rings in Zones 1 and 2
95 Fire detection wiring

Hawker Siddeley 748

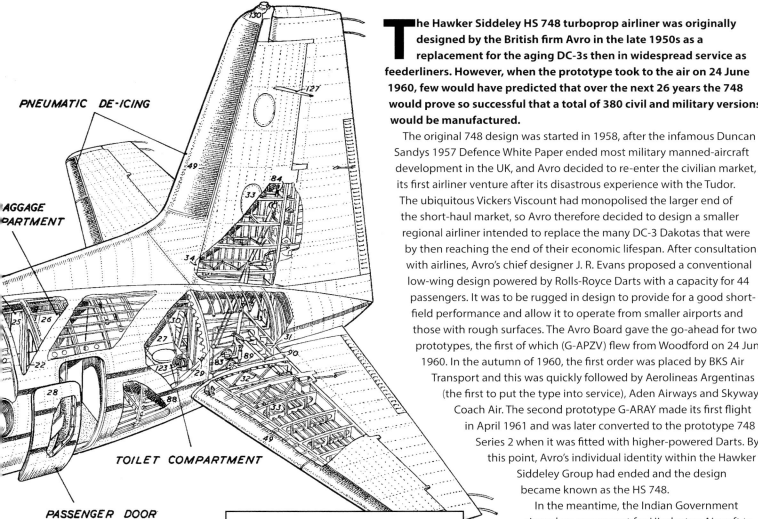

PNEUMATIC DE-ICING

AGGAGE
PARTMENT

TOILET COMPARTMENT

PASSENGER DOOR

EN SEAT ROWS

WING INCLINED JET PIPE

S PARTIALLY EXTENDED

The Hawker Siddeley HS 748 turboprop airliner was originally designed by the British firm Avro in the late 1950s as a replacement for the aging DC-3s then in widespread service as feederliners. However, when the prototype took to the air on 24 June 1960, few would have predicted that over the next 26 years the 748 would prove so successful that a total of 380 civil and military versions would be manufactured.

The original 748 design was started in 1958, after the infamous Duncan Sandys 1957 Defence White Paper ended most military manned-aircraft development in the UK, and Avro decided to re-enter the civilian market, its first airliner venture after its disastrous experience with the Tudor. The ubiquitous Vickers Viscount had monopolised the larger end of the short-haul market, so Avro therefore decided to design a smaller regional airliner intended to replace the many DC-3 Dakotas that were by then reaching the end of their economic lifespan. After consultation with airlines, Avro's chief designer J. R. Evans proposed a conventional low-wing design powered by Rolls-Royce Darts with a capacity for 44 passengers. It was to be rugged in design to provide for a good short-field performance and allow it to operate from smaller airports and those with rough surfaces. The Avro Board gave the go-ahead for two prototypes, the first of which (G-APZV) flew from Woodford on 24 June 1960. In the autumn of 1960, the first order was placed by BKS Air Transport and this was quickly followed by Aerolineas Argentinas (the first to put the type into service), Aden Airways and Skyways Coach Air. The second prototype G-ARAY made its first flight in April 1961 and was later converted to the prototype 748 Series 2 when it was fitted with higher-powered Darts. By this point, Avro's individual identity within the Hawker Siddeley Group had ended and the design became known as the HS 748.

In the meantime, the Indian Government signed an agreement for Hindustan Aircraft to build 748s at Kanpur. The first Indian-assembled aircraft flew at the end of 1961, with 90 produced for the Indian AF and Indian Airlines.

By 1967 the Series 2A was introduced which, again, was the same basic aircraft but with Mk 532 engines and a further increase in gross weight. From 1971 on, a large freight door in the rear cabin and strengthened cabin floor were offered as options on the Series 2A. Just as the Avro 748 had become the Hawker Siddeley 748, with the nationalisation (and later privatisation) of British Aerospace in 1977, it was rebranded again as the BAe 748.

In a competitive market place, development had to continue and the basis for the BAe 748 Series 2B was the uprated Dart 536 with 2,280hp fitted with 12ft propellers. Wingspan was extended by 4ft and it also featured a modernised passenger cabin, improvements to the fuel, water methanol injection system, and engine fire protection systems.

Production of the 748 ended in 1988, by which time 380 were produced (including the Andover).

HS 748 Series 2B

Crew:	Three (two pilots and one passenger attendant)
Capacity:	40–58 passengers
Payload:	11,323lb (5,136kg)
Length:	67ft (20.42m)
Wingspan:	102ft 5½in (31.23m)
Height:	24ft 10in (7.57m)
Wing area:	829ft^2 (77m^2)
Empty weight:	27,126lb (12,327kg)
Max. take-off weight:	46,500lb (21,092kg)
Powerplant:	2 × Rolls-Royce Dart RDa.7 Mk 536-2 turboprop, 2,280ehp (1,700kW) each
Cruise speed:	281mph (452km/h)
Range:	1,066 miles (1,715km) (with max payload)
Service ceiling:	25,000ft (7,620m)

Still in service worldwide today, typical passenger seating in the 748 is for 40-48 economy class seats (four abreast), however most are operated as quick change combis, with a movable bulkhead dividing the main cabin into two, with anywhere from four to 40 seats in the rear section and cargo in the forward section. The 748 is also widely used as a pure freighter with a typical max payload of about 12,000lb. In keeping with its original ethos as a DC-3 replacement, it is still popular with a variety of airlines operating in remote areas, thanks to its ability to haul payloads of over 10,000lb in and out of short rough fields with little to no ground service equipment.

Below: An unpainted HS 748 Series 2A, G-AZJH, demonstrating its large freight door in the rear cabin. The rugged performance of the 748 was accomplished by a long, high-lift wing and a unique single slot flap with a hinged flap tab at the trailing edge. The wing was mounted low on the fuselage with dihedral from the root, allowing good overall ground clearance and easy mounting of strong durable landing gear. Other features of the 748 included an internal engine starting system, and systems and structures that were designed to be easy to inspect and repair in the field with limited equipment.

*Left: **The first order for the Avro 748 was received from BKS Air Transport. The Avro 748 was an economical feederliner intended for hot and high operations around the world. The basic price for a new Avro 748 Series 1 in 1960 was £176,000, with the corresponding 748 Series 2 being £196,000.***

*Below: **A pair of 748s under construction at Woodford. Eventually 380 of the type would emerge from production lines in the UK and India.***

BAe ATP

Reflecting the strength and versatility of the original Avro design, British Aerospace decided to produce a larger aircraft with a minimum of changes to be designated ATP (Advanced Turboprop). The ATP could accommodate 72 rather than its predecessor's 44/52 passengers, which was achieved by lengthening the fuselage by 16ft fore and aft of the wing. Pratt & Whitney Canada PW124s were chosen to power distinctive custom-designed, slow-turning, six-blade propellers developed by Hamilton Standard. The combination proved to be remarkably quiet and fuel efficient. A sharper nose and swept back tail completed the new look. The aircraft first flew in August 1986 and entered service with British Midland in 1988.

The ATP featured an advanced electronic flight instrument system flight deck, and retained the type's good short-field performance. In total 64 aircraft were assembled at BAe's Woodford and Prestwick facilities with the manufacture of the airframe and wings undertaken at Chadderton. Production ended at Prestwick in 1996.

*Above: **Resplendent in British Aerospace colours, the 748 Series 2B prototype G-BGJV first took to the air on 22 June 1979. Its extended wingtips are clearly visible. In later life it served with the Sri Lankan Air Force, but had the unfortunate distinction of being shot down by a SAM missile fired by Tamil separatists.***

*Left: **British Airways 748 Series 2A entered service with the airline in 1975 and provided many years of sterling service. The type was finally retired from operation with the national carrier in 1989.***

*Right: **The cockpit of the HS 748 was typical of airliners of its time, complete with ashtrays for the pilots!***

Andover

Hawker Siddeley used the HS 748 as the base for its HS 780 Andover, a transport aircraft built for the Royal Air Force. The HS 780s were essentially 748s but with a redesigned rear fuselage and empennage which included a large rear loading ramp and a squatting main landing gear to allow fast and easy loading of large freight items.

The first production Andover C1 flew from Woodford on 9 July 1965 and the first four aircraft were used for trials and tests with both Hawker Siddeley and the Aeroplane & Armament Experimental Establishment at Boscombe Down. Following a release to service in May 1966, the fifth production aircraft was delivered to No 46 Squadron at RAF Abingdon in June 1966. Subsequent RAF types were the Andover CC2 VIP transport and Andover E3 electronic calibration aircraft.

*Above: **The Andover was the militarised variant of the HS 748. The aircraft had larger four-bladed propellers than the 748, which required a greater distance between the engines and the fuselage, although the wingtips were reduced by 18in to maintain the same wingspan as the 748. A dihedral tailplane was also fitted to keep it clear of the propeller slipstream. Following a release to service in May 1966 the fifth production aircraft was delivered in June 1966.***

*Top centre: **The first prototype G-APZV was converted to become the aerodynamic prototype of the 748 Military Freighter with a rear tail and rear-opening doors to allow for air dropping and straight in loading. It was re-registered G-ARRV and flew in this guise on 21 December 1963.***

*Top right and right: **With rear doors open, RAF Andover C1 XS603 is seen demonstrating its air dropping capability. The aircraft was later converted into an E3 variant and operated by No 115 Squadron based at RAF Brize Norton (later RAF Benson), operating Andovers (replacing the Armstrong Whitworth AW660 Argosy) from 1976 in the radio aids calibration role.***

Shorts Skyvan

Affectionately called 'the shed' by its pilots for obvious reasons, the Shorts SC7 Skyvan was a utility aircraft that found its niche as a short-haul freighter and skydiving platform. A child of the 1960s, it spawned the equally successful Shorts 330 and 360 regional airliners.

The Shorts SC7 Skyvan had its origins in the Miles Aerovan, the concept of which was taken on by Shorts in a radically overhauled design. Shorts built a comparatively low-cost aircraft of functional construction, a twin-engined all-metal design with a braced, high aspect ratio wing, and an unpressurised, square-section fuselage. Most notably it had a beaver tail with twin fins allowing for loading through a ramp in the upward sloping rear fuselage. Construction started at Sydenham Airport in 1960 and the prototype first flew on 17 January 1963, powered by Continental piston engines, but it was decided that turboprop power was required, so the prototype and early production (Series 2) examples were fitted with Astazou II turboprops. These engines were not ideal for hot-and-high conditions, so the Series 3 was upgraded with Garrett AiResearch TPE-331-201 turboprops.

The first Skyvan delivery was made to AerAlpi in Italy in 1966 and others soon followed to Emerald Airways, Ansett-MAL and Northern Consolidated of Alaska, amongst others. In all, 149 Skyvans were built and sold to commercial freight/passenger 'bush' operators and military/paramilitary organisations. The type remained in service into the second decade of the 21st century, with both civil and military operators.

*Above: **The Shorts Skyvan prototype, G-ASCN, re-engined with turboprop Turbomeca Astazou 2 engines, with which it first flew on 2 October 1962. Skyvan trials continued until its last flight on 15 August 1966. The aircraft was scrapped 10 years later.***

Production ended in 1986 folllowing the launch of its extended-fuselage commuterliner successors, the Shorts 330 and Shorts 360.

Shorts Skyvan 3

Crew:	One-two
Capacity:	19 passengers
Length:	40ft 1in (12.21m)
Wingspan:	64ft 11in (19.78m)
Height:	15ft 1in (4.6m)
Empty weight:	7,344lb (3,331kg)
Max. take-off weight:	12,500lb (5,670kg)
Powerplant:	2 × Garrett AiResearch TPE-331-201 turboprops, 715shp each
Maximum speed:	202mph (325km/h)
Cruise speed:	197mph (317km/h)
Range:	694 miles (1,117km)
Service ceiling:	22,500ft (6,858m)
Rate of climb:	1,640ft/min (500m/min)

Shorts Belfast

Although the military-designed Belfast might not immediately be considered a 'propliner', in later life it carved out a civil career for itself as an out-sized cargo carrier with HeavyLift Cargo Airlines. As such, it was the largest propeller-driven aircraft ever to enter service with a British carrier and is a fitting finale to our 'classic' collection.

A giant of an aircraft, the Shorts Belfast was developed to meet Air Staff Requirement 371 for a freighter capable of carrying a wide range of military loads over a long range. Shorts' design was based on studies it had worked on in the late 1950s as the SC5/10. To meet the demands of the specification the Belfast used a high wing carrying four Rolls-Royce Tyne turboprops. The cargo deck,

64ft long in a fuselage over 18ft in diameter (roomy enough for two single deck buses), was reached through a 'beaver tail' with rear loading doors and integral ramp. The main undercarriage was two eight-wheel bogies and a two-wheel nose. The Belfast was capable of an impressive maximum take-off weight of over 220,500lb (100 tonnes) and could carry 150 troops with full equipment, or a Chieftain

tank or two Westland Wessex helicopters. The prototype first flew on 5 January 1964 with chief test pilot Denis Taylor at the controls, but the euphoria did not last long when the RAF requirement for 30 aircraft was reduced to just 10 as an economic measure stemming from the UK's Sterling Crisis of 1965. The Belfast C1, as it was designated, entered service with No 53 Squadron in January 1966 based at RAF Fairford. Major drag problems prevented the first five aircraft from reaching the desired performance and modifications including the addition of a new rear fairing were necessary to improve cruising speed to the required level – by which time the unfortunate sobriquets of 'Dragmaster' and 'Belslow' had been acquired. Worse was to follow. The reorganisation of the RAF and introduction of Strike Command in 1968 heralded the retirement of several aircraft types including the Britannia and Comet in 1975 and the Belfast the following year. By the end of 1976 the Belfast fleet had been retired.

Heavylift (then TAC Heavylift) acquired five Belfasts for commercial service in 1977, and three were placed into service in 1980. Marshalls of Cambridge performed a number of modifications on the Belfast which allowed it to be certificated to civil standards. Ironically, the RAF chartered these aircraft to support the airlift commitment during the Falklands War in 1982 and a single machine in support of the First Gulf War almost a decade later. The last remaining Belfast was flown to Australia in 2003 where it saw out its days.

*Below: **Gentle giant. The Belfast in its civil guise with Transmeridian Air Cargo, fulfilled a niche market for outsize airfreight. TAC was a British cargo airline that operated from 1962 until 1979 when it merged with IAS Cargo Airlines to form Heavylift Cargo Airlines. G-BEPS was one of three Belfasts that it flew for over a decade until the aircraft became uneconomical to operate.***

Left: Resembling a Hercules on steroids, the Belfast was a four-engined heavy transport for the RAF, the first of which flew on 5 January 1964. When it first entered service the type experienced heavy drag problems that severely curtailed its speed and range and was often nicknamed the 'Dragmaster'. Although the issue was largely corrected it was stuck with the stigma throughout the rest of its service career.

Bottom left: The first Belfast to fly was XR362 for the RAF and was named Samson. It briefly carried the civil registration G-ASKE during overseas test flights. It later became G-BEPE with HeavyLift but was ultimately scrapped.

Above right: With its propellers squeezing moisture out of the overcast conditions, an RAF Belfast gets air under its tyres as the aircraft thunders down the runway.

Right: An impressive demonstration of the Belfast's lifting capability as three British Army Saladin armoured cars disembark. It was specifically designed for the carriage of heavy freight, including the largest types of guns, vehicles, guided missiles and other loads and had 'beaver-tail' rear loading doors capable of permitting the unhindered passage of any load that the fuselage could contain. As a troop transport it could carry 200 men, and was often used to carry helicopters overseas.

Below: The Belfast provided sterling service for RAF Transport Command over its 10 years of service, a role that it was to reprieve during the Falklands War when the aircraft it sold to HeavyLift were chartered back by the service.

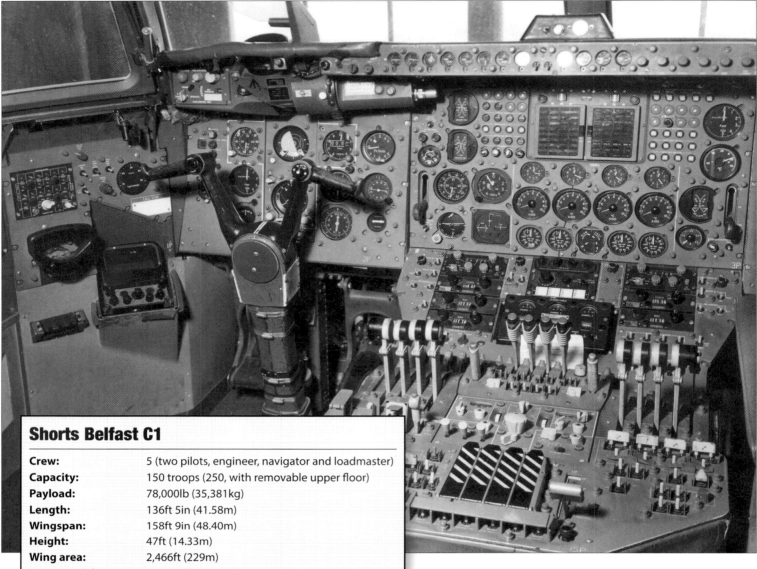

Shorts Belfast C1

Crew:	5 (two pilots, engineer, navigator and loadmaster)
Capacity:	150 troops (250, with removable upper floor)
Payload:	78,000lb (35,381kg)
Length:	136ft 5in (41.58m)
Wingspan:	158ft 9in (48.40m)
Height:	47ft (14.33m)
Wing area:	2,466ft (229m)
Empty weight:	127,000lb (57,607kg)
Max. take-off weight:	230,000lb (104,328kg)
Powerplant:	4 × Rolls-Royce Tyne R.Ty.12, Mk101 turboprop, 5,730 ehp each
Top speed:	352mph (566 km/h)
Cruise speed:	336mph (541km/h) at 24,000ft (7,315m)
Range:	5,300 miles (8,528 km) with maximum fuel. 1,000 miles (1,609 km) with maximum payload
Service ceiling:	30,000ft (9,144m)
Rate of climb:	1,060ft/min (5.4 m/s)

*Above: **The front office of the Belfast provided its pilots with a spacious work place. The Belfast was notable for being the second aircraft built equipped with autoland blind landing equipment.***

*Right: **The Rolls-Royce Tyne was often considered to be underpowered for an aircraft of the size of the Belfast, but it was nevertheless a good airlifter and was able to fly to Akrotiri in Cyprus with a load of two Wessex.***

*Below: **Belfast XR365 was given the name Hector by the RAF and later became G-HLFT when in service with HeavyLift Cargo Airlines.***
Andy Hay/www.flyinagart.co.uk

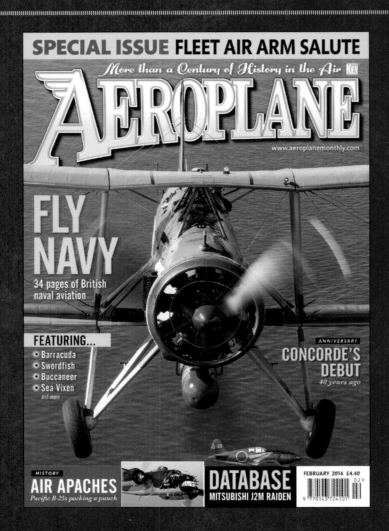